REFLECTIONS
on the pool

PHOTOGRAPHS BY MELBA LEVICK

TEXT BY CLEO BALDON AND IB MELCHIOR

REFLECTIONS
on the pool
CALIFORNIA DESIGNS FOR SWIMMING

Rizzoli
NEW YORK

To my Mother and Father —ML

To Sid Galper—CB

In photographing this book I owe thanks to all the people who so generously opened their
pools to us, as well as to the talented architects and designers whose wonderful ideas fill these pages.

I also wish to express gratitude to my agent and friend, Sarah Jane Freyman. For many years
I have appreciated and benefited from her excellent counsel and unfailing support.

—Melba Levick

Special thanks to: Michael Buccino, landscape architect; Mark Francis, University of California
at Davis; Elliott Gottfurcht, builder; Grace Hall, assistant to Tommy Church; Jeff Hyland,
realtor and Beverly Hills historian; Susan Kaufman, realtor; Michael Laurie, University of California,
Berkeley; Berna Linden, realtor; and Lyman Scheel, pool builder.

—Cleo Baldon, Ib Melchior

First published in the United States of America in 1997 by
Rizzoli International Publications, Inc.
300 Park Avenue South, New York, NY 10010

Library of Congress Cataloging-in-Publication Data
Baldon, Cleo.
  Reflections on the pool/ text by Cleo Baldon &
Ib Melchior; photographs by Melba Levick.
     p.   cm.
  ISBN 0-8478-2014-9
  1. Swimming pools. I. Melchior, Ib. II. Levick, Melba.
III. Title.
TH4763.B35 1997
728'.9—dc20   96-44236
                         CIP

Designed by Sisco & Evans, New York

Photography credits: page 162: © Hearst San Simeon State Historical Monument— All Rights Reserved. Photo: Doug Allen
page 164: Photograph by William Randolph Harrison. Used with permission of Elliot Gottfurcht.

Frontispiece: A reflection is used as a design element in Sonoma (see p. 100)
page 6: The Donnell pool, Sonoma (see p. 172)
page 11: A striped weir quotes the columns of the facade in Encino (see p. 86)

Printed and bound in Great Britain

CONTENTS

INTRODUCTION

Swimming pools are oases for relaxation, fun, and exercise that range from highly ornamented, luxurious havens to serene, almost Zen styles. Nowhere are pools more picture perfect or imaginatively designed than in California. In California the swimming pool offers a distinct way of life in which the pool area is an extension of the regular living space, and the climate allows indoor and outdoor activities to mingle. It is perhaps for this reason that California has more private, in-ground swimming pools—at last count 820,000—than any other state.

Not only does California have the right climate to take the greatest advantage of pools, but unlike other warm places, California's diverse environments encourage a wide variety of picturesque pools—in the hot desert sands of Palm Springs and Mohave; the craggy rocks and sandy beaches of Big Sur and Carmel; the cool trees of Big Bear and the Sierras; the verdant vineyards of Sonoma and Napa Valley; the mountains of Yosemite and Sequoia; the green fields of the Imperial Valley, and the opulent estates of Beverly Hills and Piedmont. In this respect California is unique. No other place in the country can offer such a variety of terrain into which to carve an enchanting pool. In this environment, pool design has evolved from the basic to the spectacular.

The ancestor of the modern swimming pool is the ancient bath, a basin of any size large enough for the immersion of the entire body in water. Baths or pools existed in the gardens of wealthy nobles in Egypt more than three thousand years ago, in the Valley of the Indus in India, as well as in the early Persian, Moorish, and Byzantine civilizations, but the remains of these pools are too fragmented to permit detailed reconstruction. A spectacular exception is the Great Bath at Mohenjo-daro in Pakistan, excavated in the 1920s, with large pools that are still well preserved after five thousand years.

Baths and pools occupied an important place in early Greece, where the inability to swim was the mark of an uneducated person. Roman baths and swimming pools still exist, such as the impressive pools at Hadrian's Villa near Rome, which dates to c. 129 CE, and the astonishingly sophisticated baths and pools at Pompeii. Rome in particular boasted hundreds of bathing establishments, which included steam baths as well as large swimming pools with either hot or cold water.

The famed pool at Masada near the Dead Sea in today's Israel dates back to before the beginning of the Common Era. Gouged out of the bedrock on a mountain top, the pool is complete with individual niches or "lockers" hewn out of the surrounding rock walls, where the swimmers could store their clothing while they used the pool. It was excavated in 1963–65 and today it is a popular tourist attraction.

Swimming pools and baths, both public and private, continued their development in the east and the west, gradually reaching Europe. In the 1850s the concept of swimming pools was brought to England from India and Japan, and their use spread rapidly. Most baths and pools in England were indoors and public, and they soon attained unequaled architectural grandeur and spectacular proportions.

In the United States, the first public pool, or municipal pool as it was called, was probably the one built in Brookline, Massachusetts in 1887, and soon thereafter other cities such as New York and Chicago followed suit. The public pool in California was represented around the turn of the century by such enormous natatoria as the impressive Venice Plunge in Venice, California. This pool was built in 1905 by A. R. Fraser as part of a complex envisioned by Abbott Kinney, based loosely on the canals and buildings of Venice, Italy. The Sutro Baths in San Francisco, built in 1894, comprised seven huge swimming pools in a two-acre complex filled with recreational equipment. Swimmers could rent a suit, cap, and towel for a quarter. The foundations of the baths still lie on the shore of San Francisco near the Cliff House restaurant and Seal Rock.

By 1920 the swimming pool had come into its own, and a decade later, residential pools, then called estate pools, proliferated throughout the country.

Architectural tradition, garden design, and therefore pool styles in California differ from those of the Midwest and the East. The Spanish settlements in the eighteenth century, which influenced mission-style architecture, and the prosperity of the 1920s, which led to imported Italian villa designs, Renaissance-style terraces, and classical details, left their marks on the unique array of California regional styles. The style of swimming pools followed suit. In the 1920s for instance, many pools were modeled after the reflecting pools and channels of European traditional gardens. Modern architecture of the early twentieth century propagated swimming pools of its own style. Both Frank Lloyd Wright's Ennis Brown house and pool of 1924, and the Lovell Health House of 1927 by Richard Neutra, with the pool built into a terrace as part of the house, still survive on the hills above Los Angeles.

These early residential pools were status symbols of the very wealthy—desirable but inaccessible to most because of the cost of construction. This involved building a form of plywood or fiberglass to hold poured concrete, or constructing a shell of reinforced concrete blocks. In 1940 the gunite method of constructing private swimming pools came into use, superseding the poured-in-place method, and pool ownership became possible for nearly everyone who owned a house with enough space. Gunite is a stiff, fast-setting mix of concrete and sand that is sprayed onto the pool framework and hardens almost on contact, making forms and containers unnecessary.

With gunite available, swimming pools became an integral part of the new California landscape design that promoted the creation of gardens and outdoor spaces for better living. Landscape architect Thomas Church (1902–1978) is credited with contributing much to this new approach, especially with his 1955 book *Gardens Are for People*. His widely published Donnell pool of 1948 in the San Francisco Bay area influenced generations of pool designers with its curved shapes, and probably fathered the ubiquitous and often clumsy kidney-shaped pool.

Hollywood has had a distinct influence on the popularity of the California swimming pool all over the world. By presenting such sights as Esther Williams displaying her swimming skills in dozens of motion pictures in the 1940s and 1950s, or a bevy of Valley Girls romping in the water with their sun-bronzed dates, Hollywood films created an association in the American mind between the glamor of Hollywood stars and the California swimming pool.

Family gatherings, weddings, anniversaries, and other memorable events have taken place around the swimming pool in films such as *The Graduate* (1967) in which the title character played by Dustin Hoffman tries his new scuba gear in the pool. Cars, bikes, horses, and dogs have landed in pools over the years. Even an elephant took the plunge in *The Party* (1968) with Peter Sellers. And as *Sunset Boulevard* opens, a dead body is found in the pool. The legendary pool at Pickfair, the home of Mary Pickford and Douglas Fairbanks Sr., was large enough to hold a canoe in which Mary and Doug would paddle back and forth. Today, recently renovated, the pool at Pickfair holds a large, bright yellow rubber raft instead of a canoe.

As the sparkle of Hollywood made residential pools more desirable, the growing availability of the gunite process of construction and the development of other pool conveniences made pool ownership and maintenance relatively easy. Today's pool construction involves only ten steps.

First, a hole of the desired shape and size is excavated, then all plumbing and electrical lines are installed. An interlaced framework of iron reinforcement bars, or re-bars, lashed together, is formed along the inside of the excavation. Gunite is sprayed under high pressure onto this framework to the desired thickness, usually about ten inches, and the bondbeam—the top edging of the pool—is formed. The deck material connecting to the bondbeam is put in place, then the tile or stone edging inside the pool is completed. Every pool must have this edging three to four inches above and below the water's surface, or the plaster will crack due to the difference in air and water temperatures. Next the pool pumping, filtering, and heating equipment is connected. This equipment is usually housed in a shed or enclosure out of sight. Before plaster is applied to the pool, any desired landscaping close to the pool is done so soil will not stick to the plaster, and the required security fence is erected. The gunite is then surfaced with plaster mixed to the desired color. In California many pools are black for maximum reflecting capacity, so they act like giant mirrors. Black pools also stay about five degrees warmer than pools of a lighter color. Finally, immediately after plastering, the pool is filled with water. This must be done quickly, or the plaster may overdry and crack.

In some instances the water with which the pool is filled comes from a private well on the property, but usually it comes from the municipal supply. One cannot pull a plug to drain pools to make repairs, perform a thorough cleaning, or to prevent the pool from freezing and cracking in areas where the winter gets cold. In these cases, the pool must be emptied with a pump, or simply heated to keep it from freezing.

Special equipment developed in the 1950s and 1960s such as heaters, underwater lighting, and auto-fill sensors and valves are now standard in many pools. Skimmers and filters draw debris from the water and the clean water is recirculated into the pool. Most pool owners pay a professional who regularly services the pool and, when necessary, adds chlorine to kill bacteria and algae. He also cleans the filter traps and tests the pH balance to keep the pool fit for healthy use. Some pools have covers, which keep the water warm and prevent debris from falling into the pool.

The style and design of a pool is its most noticeable feature, and there are two categories of residential pools, although these categories sometimes overlap. The first category includes pools that architecturally complement the houses at which they are built. These pools tend to have more formal lines, with underwater access steps and a polished design approach featuring water weirs, fountains, raised seating edges, and bright-hued flowers and plants in ornamental pots placed on the deck. In the second category, pools that are nature-inspired emulate natural settings with rocks and boulders, landscaped rock formations with waterfalls, gradual beach entries, and overhanging trees.

Each pool must, of course, take design cues from the desires of the owners and the features of the adjoining house and land. There are myriad ways of combining features to achieve an effect. The innovative possibilities are often at their best in the sensational spectrum of California pools.

But whatever form a pool takes, it has one further important aspect that reaches us on an emotional level. We are drawn to water. We seek to live beside it, at streams and rivers, oceans and lakes. We can imagine the pool as a link to our primordial past; pools respond to a profound emotional need and satisfy it.

The natural pool imitates the appearance of ponds or water holes found in nature. It is usually surrounded by vegetation native to the area where the pool is built, with additional flowers and shrubbery that complement and blend with existing plants and trees, and come right to the water's edge.

The natural pool should look as if it had been discovered rather than designed; nature itself should be the model. Thus natural pools tend to be constructed farther away from the residence than other pools. The irregular shape of the natural pool makes it appear to have flowed into a depression in the land. The design should be such that aside from the natural bends, spurs, and inlets there is an adequate, straight stretch for unencumbered swimming, with minimum dimensions of nine by thirty feet.

Natural pools are usually surrounded by boulders and rocks that rise to various heights above the water line and descend deep into the water as in nature. The rocks are often found on the site and are supplemented with artificial rocks that are impossible to discern from the real ones in appearance and to the touch. The construction of these artificial rocks is an intricate process. After the desired shapes and sizes are chosen, latex impressions of actual boulders and rock formations are made. The "rocks" are then cast in light-weight concrete over a fiberglass form, textured and painted with a wear-proof and waterproof paint to

look exactly like the real rock, and finally incorporated with real boulders and rocks to form a rockscape. Artificial boulders and rocks can also be hand-shaped on site with the same result. The benefit of using artificial rocks is that they are lightweight and can be created in specific sizes and shapes. This becomes especially important when selecting rocks that will be underwater. They can be L-shaped, resting on the rim of the pool with one part dipping into the water to create the appearance of being naturally embedded in the edge. Underwater, the gunite and plaster shell must remain inviolate to prevent leakage, so rocks cannot be set into the pool wall, but a shelf can be attached to the poolside underwater, onto which a natural boulder can be fastened.

Artificial rocks can also be affixed to the surface of the pool wall, appearing to penetrate it without doing so.

Access to the pool can take the form of underwater rock steps or a natural beach ramp of plain, textured plaster and concrete, or concrete inset with pebbles, flagstones, or sand.

Often, a waterfall, which can range from an eight-foot cascade to a trickle meandering through the boulders, helps create a natural look. The water is recirculated from the pool itself, and the hollow rocks allow the concealment of water lines and the pump system, including the

reservoir which forms the top lip of the fall. This reservoir is a container made of metal or plastic which is filled with water from the pool by the pump. The wall of this container that faces the pool is lower than the others, allowing the water to spill over into channels designated by the placement of rocks for the descent. Pockets can be fashioned in the artificial boulders to hold native shrubs, grasses, and small plants to heighten the natural feeling of the man-made haven.

CHAPTER ONE

THE NATURAL POOL

THE NATURAL POOL: MONTECITO

I n Montecito, a beautiful, rock-ringed swimming pool has been placed
in a woodland setting so closely wedded to nature that a pair of wild ducks
mistook it for the real thing.

The Japanese-style pool pavilion and the stepping stones framed by Korean grass give the setting a Far Eastern mood.

In Montecito, a beautiful, rock-ringed swimming pool has been placed in a woodland setting so closely wedded to nature that a pair of wild ducks mistook it for the real thing. The fluffy ducklings that later appeared testify to the successful styling of natural elements, which combine the charm of a cottage garden and the natural beauty of a woodland glade.

The pool was designed in 1978 by Isabelle Greene, today one of California's most prominent landscape architects. It was her first swimming pool, and today it is a showcase for her hallmark natural aesthetics. Greene designs pools in many styles, though, and the owners of this pool did not specifically request a natural design. Their home is English-style, with wide, sloping lawns spilling down toward a wooded area, and here—at the edge of the woods a short walk from the house—Greene planned a pool to take advantage of the idyllic setting.

The shape of the pool was designed to skirt the drip line of a grove of oak trees at the site. The boulders and rocks that form the pool's edge and dot the area around it were excavated on-site as the pool was built. A six-ton boulder that could not be removed even by a truck and crane was instead maneuvered, by use of a dirt ramp, into a position where it appears to be part of the natural pool rim. Two large boulders at the deep end of the pool are positioned as diving platforms. Boulders also can be seen below the water's surface, creating intriguing forms and shadows in the approximately twenty-by-sixty-foot pool. The black plaster lining of the pool creates a natural-looking reflection on the water of the surrounding trees and plants.

To complement the existing vegetation of the wooded area, Greene brought in dogwoods and columbine and the Korean grass ground cover which pushes up between the flagstones of the decking area and smothers the small boulders around the pool. This grass resists the adverse effects of the chlorinated water. Extra-strong skimmers circulate the water and keep the surface clean of the above-average amount of debris that lands in the pool. A gas heater keeps the pool at swimming temperature all year, causing a bewitching mist to rise over it on frosty mornings. The equipment is housed in a bunker dug into the slope of the hill, where it cannot be seen or heard.

Ten years after the pool was constructed, the owners asked Greene to select the site for a pool house and choose an architect and contractor with whom to work to maintain the integrity of the pool in the design of the new structure. The result was a Japanese-style pavilion with an *endawa*, a raised wooden deck, all around it, *soji* screens, handmade rubbed wood detailing, and a slate roof. From this poolside pavilion, the owners host a yearly dance event, which of course ends with all the dancers in the pool!

Like her grandfather, arts-and-crafts architect Henry Greene, Isabelle Greene lets natural elements express their inherent beauty.

THE NATURAL POOL: CARMICHAEL

There is a saying among landscape designers that the buyer

of the rocks should never be the one to place them, since a natural look

depends on burying much of the investment underground.

Man-made areas such as the flagstone and redwood decking (left) should look distinct from the "natural" elements at water's edge.

Completed in 1985 after three and a half years of construction, this natural pool is made of over three hundred boulders and rocks.

The owner purchased several lots in a wooded area of this Sacramento suburb, until he had a property of four acres. He then bought additional acreage some distance away for the boulders and rocks scattered about there. The rocks were trucked to the pool site, and when the acreage had been cleared of rocks, the enterprising owner sold it as farm land to defray his costs.

Landscape architect Michael Glassman shaped the pool shell with a notched bondbeam that incorporates underwater shelving to support the huge boulders, which weigh up to eight tons each. For three days Glassman supervised the placement of the rocks that would form the rim of the pool, positioning them to dip down into the water as they would in nature. Other rocks placed in hap-hazard order around the pool site seem to be natural outcroppings; many of the boulders are almost buried in the ground and are covered with lichen and moss. Care must be taken to cover rocks and boulders partially with water or earth, or they will look like potatoes about to roll off the site. There is a saying among landscape designers that the buyer of the rocks should never be the one to place them, since a natural look depends on burying much of the investment underground.

Two topiary trees frame a glimpse of water beyond a narrow bridge, partially obscuring the water's edge and increasing the feeling of space.

The forty-five-by-twenty-five-foot pool itself is plastered directly to the rocks in the rim and on the shelves, and is dark gray. The pool has no heating system because the dark color absorbs heat from the sun all day, and on a summer's day the air temperature can reach well over a hundred degrees.

Unlike most pools, this one does not have chlorinated water, but instead contains a sophisticated water purification system. The water is pumped through oversized pipes past a series of ultraviolet lights that kill bacteria (including streptococci, which chlorine does not kill) and allow vegetation such as lichen and moss to reach down to the water unharmed. The system also includes ozonators to introduce oxygen into the water, much as in tropical fish tanks.

The house appears to be an old country lodge, but in fact was built at the same time as the pool. Together they seem to have inhabited the site for years, nestled among valley oaks, blue oaks, pin oaks, and crepe myrtle.

The spa is fed by two small waterfalls
and overflows in three more falls
into the pool.

The entry to the pool is a sandy, beach-like ramp designed at a slope
that is safe for wading into the water. Birds, raccoons, and deer
wade here, and drink where they can reach
the water's surface.

A natural pool should look like a body
of water filling a natural depression
in the landscape. This concept is reinforced
here with a sandy, beach-like entrance
to the pool.

Designed by noted landscape architect
Isabelle Greene, and built in 1983 on a
three-acre ranch in the Santa Ynez
Mountains, this pool has an unusual
feature that gives it a look of added
authenticity over other natural pools.

Instead of conventional steps, the entry
to the pool is a sandy, beach-like ramp
designed at a slope that is safe for wading
into the water. Nestled between the rocks,
it takes up the entire space of one end of
the pool. The sand is actually an aggregate
of small stones set in a polymer resin.
Birds, raccoons, and deer wade here, and
drink where they can reach the water,
and even an occasional wild boar has been
known to use the sandy slope. The boars
are less welcome, however, since they have
a tendency to root up the lawn.

The owners chose this free-form pool
without hard lines as the design best
suited to the site. The forty-by-fifteen-
foot pool with dark blue plaster is located
in a small gully about forty feet from the
house. A short distance from the pool
is a spa—a small, rock-embraced water
hole which appears to be spring fed by a

small waterfall. As the runoff flows down
the gully, it seems to be part of the same
water course as the swimming pool.

The rolling hills of the ranch are sparse-
ly dotted with oak trees and covered with
native grasses that turn golden-yellow
by late summer, giving California its
nickname—The Golden State. In the
area around the gully, the pool, and
the spa grows Korean grass, its unruly
blades poking out in every direction like
cowlicks. There are fescue and columbine, German irises, and Santa Barbara
daisies in pockets among the rocks.
Spikes of wild-looking yarrow complete
the setting of this "native" pond.

Propane-heated, and serviced in the
normal manner, the Santa Ynez pool only
once posed a maintenance problem—
when torrential rains turned the little
gully into a raging stream that dumped
several inches of sediment in the pool.
The clean-up was considerable!

The clients wanted to take advantage of the spectacular expanse
of the golf course, making it their own and lending visual drama
to the pool setting.

The waterfall through the rocks into the pool seems to originate in the golf course lake, and makes the pool and the background appear to be one continuous landscape.

Indian Wells is an opulent desert community near Palm Springs at the foot of the San Jacinto Mountains in Riverside County. With a mean daytime desert temperature of eighty-nine degrees, Palm Springs and Indian Wells abound with swimming pools. One of the most pleasing and imaginative of these is located in the gated Vintage Club development.

Custom built for the present owners in 1995, the residence was designed by architect Tom Jakway and the pool was designed by Wayne C. Connors & Associates, a firm that had been recommended to them by both their contractor and their interior designer.

The clients wanted a pool in which they could cool off during the seasonal desert heat, which would also provide a strong garden element of natural beauty. The property on which the pool was to be built bordered the development's golf course and lake, and the clients wanted to take advantage of this spectacular expanse, making it their own and lending visual drama to the pool setting, which offers a view of Mount Eisenhower in the distance.

The landscaping at the pool's edge
is in harmony with the forms of the rolling
countryside beyond.

The resulting pool, a luxurious oasis, sits on the property border between the house and the golf course. The pool is rectangular, with its long side designed to follow the property line. At its longest it is thirty-nine feet, and at its widest, eighteen feet, and it is constructed with gunite and gray plaster. At the pool edge closest to the house, the stone patio partially covered by a columned portico brings the pool area right up to the house. The rocks that line the pool on the golf course side are natural Coco Flats rocks and boulders combined with artificial rocks to match. Carefully planted with flowers and shrubs, the boulders provide privacy from the golf course side; the

small waterfall at one end of the pool seems to originate in the golf course lake beyond, and ties the landscape together.

Like all lush vegetation in this desert area, the trees, flowers and shrubbery surrounding the pool are brought to the site from other areas—even the stately palm trees that stand guard over the swimmers were specially planned for this oasis.

Boulders and plantings around the spa provide privacy from the golf course.

The Larsons realized that there were absolutely no limitations

on the design of their second pool.

A curved palm tree overhangs the entrance to this tropical oasis and an island at mid-pool lends spacial interest and suspense to what would otherwise be a large, unbroken expanse of water.

Sitting at the lush tropical pool owned by Janet and Glen Larson in Palm Springs, it is easy to imagine it as an idyllic water hole on some South Seas island. The Larson pool is a renovation left-over that became a main attraction. The original residence on the site was a hacienda built in the 1920s. In 1985 extensive remodeling was undertaken, and the Larsons decided to abandon the existing pool and build a new one ornamented with mosaic tiles on the other side of the house. This was done and plans were under way to remove and fill in the old pool, but when the shell had been removed the Larsons realized it would be a shame not to take advantage of the available excavation in such a great location, and decided to rebuild the old pool in addition to the new one. Realizing that there were absolutely no limitations on the pool's design, the Larsons created a tropical swimming hole with inlets and falls, a flagstone slope access, a mid-pool islet, and a rock grotto, all surrounded by tropical foliage. The grotto is a shaded swim-in resting place with underwater seating and a view of the islet and the spectacular curved palm tree. This palm tree was moved from the Larsons' property in Holmby Hills, probably the only palm tree transported *to* Palm Springs *from* Los Angeles!

The pool is plastered black, with wide underwater steps and ledges, including a ledge attached to the islet, as comfortable places to relax semi-submerged in the water. It is situated just off the master bedroom of the house and invites a pleasant early swim with the rising sun.

Glen Larson, a television and motion picture producer and director *(Strange Bedfellows)* has used the pool as a location for his own TV series, *PS, I Love You*, and as a tropical hotel garden restaurant, with chairs and tables with red-and-white-checkered tablecloths placed on the deck.

Although this Edenic bit of the tropics has become the main pool attraction of the Larsons' Palm Springs property, the new pool serves an important purpose— it is often designated for the children, who can splash there to the limits of their energy, leaving the luxurious, restful pool for the adults to enjoy.

Underwater ledges
provide convenient resting
places adjoining the island and
in the grotto.

Just below the house and lawn, Baldon designed a swimming pool
nestled into the artificial rocks and boulders.

A vantage point above the waterfall offers a view of the gently sloping beach access in the foreground, the generous patio, the spa, and just beyond, the roof of the play pavilion.

There was already a pool on the property when this two-story, L-shaped, contemporary house with a half-acre back yard changed hands. The new owners, however, wanted a lawn inside the L where the pool was located. They did want a pool, but the rest of the yard consisted of a precipitous slope, dropping more than thirty feet to the neighboring yard.

Designer Cleo Baldon came up with a daring and dramatic solution to the problem, allowing maximum utilization of the property with features catering both to adults and children. On the impossibly steep slope she created a magnificent natural rockscape that drops from the lawn to the yard below, and on top of this man-made mountain, just below the house and lawn, she designed a swimming pool nestled into the carefully assembled jumble of rocks and boulders. These artificial rocks, created by Di Giacomo, Inc., look and feel so real that it is impossible to distinguish them from the rocks of the High Sierras, where their impressions were taken.

The pool itself is a loosely formed L-shape that follows the contours of the rock. At the short end, a pebbled beach gradually leads into the water. The long stem of the L is forty-four feet in length for comfortable swimming, with an adjoining spa at the far end.

Looking the length of the pool from the shelter of the grotto, on the left are steps from the patio into the water, and on the far right are stairs to the deck overhead.

A passageway leads from the grotto, behind the adjoining waterfall, to a shower and dressing room.

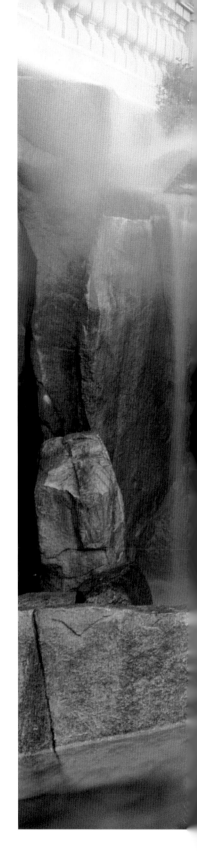

From the lawn area above, an eight-foot waterfall cascades down onto scattered rocks and flows into the pool. Above the waterfall is a fog machine which, by the turn of a handle, creates a cloud of gossamer mist that hovers over the cascading water. This fog is especially spectacular at night when beams of light shoot through it, following wisps of luminous mist that slowly dissipate into the darkness.

At the foot of the waterfall is a grotto beneath the deck of the house, with a poolside bar just above water level, and seating both in the grotto and the pool. Doors in the grotto lead to a rock-lined dressing room and shower. Chiseled into the rock wall of the dressing room passageway, a fierce, bearded Neptune keeps a watchful eye on the activities at the bar. In this tunnel there are also narrow openings behind the waterfall for viewing the pool through the cascade.

Outside, winding paths that cling to the face of the cliff descend to a garden playground below, where there is a two-story play pavilion with intricate wood carvings and a fireman's pole connecting the levels. There, a basin catches swimmers from a 150-foot water slide that runs the length of the lawn and the rockscape above.

A fog machine above the waterfall
creates a luminous mist, which is dramatically
lit at night.

As a bachelor, Norton wanted the design of the pool and pool area
to be masculine in style, almost crude. He wanted it to look
unconstructed, as though minimal work went into its creation.

A mass of natural and artificial rock rises out of the water, echoing the surrounding mountains.

In 1987 when Ken Norton built his desert home and pool in the Vintage Club development of Indian Wells, he wanted the pool to look as though he had converted a naturally occurring water hole at the base of the San Jacinto Mountains. As a bachelor, Norton wanted the design of the pool and pool area to be masculine in style, almost crude. He wanted it to look unconstructed, as though minimal work went into its creation. The appearance of the finished pool successfully belies the extraordinary efforts of building it.

Landscape architect Ron Gregory had to blast a large part of the excavation from the bedrock of the foothills. Later, he rebuilt the rock area to make it look untouched, using artificial rocks to repair the damaged natural cliff that rises out of the water on the far end of the pool. Gregory considered incorporating a waterfall in his design, but discarded the idea as too predictable.

The paving stones Norton selected for the ample deck were so rough that Gregory warned of the dangers of high heels and bruised bare feet. A few years later grout was added between the stones to help smooth the edges.

The curved access steps at the far end of the pool are tiled with penny-sized, penny-colored tiles, as is the interior of the pool. These tiles are applied directly to the gunite. The resulting earth-like color, which mimics the color of the mountains, completes the illusion of a pool that occurred naturally in the desert mountains.

In an otherwise rocky
environment, generously full,
channeled cushions provide
gracious comfort.

The pool is fifty feet at its longest
and twenty-three feet at its widest, with
a fourteen-foot narrows in the middle.

THE NATURAL POOL: SOUTH PALM SPRINGS

In the high desert of Palm Springs below the San Jacinto Mountains
a desert oasis has been created around an ambling
pueblo-style residence.

Sculptures amidst sculptural
plantings create points of interest
around the pool.

In the high desert of Palm Springs below
the San Jacinto Mountains a desert oasis
has been created around an ambling
pueblo-style residence. Here, in 1992,
landscape architect Wayne Connor
designed and built a bit of paradise for
his clients, which includes a spectacular
natural pool with two waterfalls, an exotic
Koi pond, a great lawn, a spa, a landscaped rock garden, and a hundred-foot-
long stream that meanders through
a grove of mature California fan palms
with a verdant undercover of trees and
shrubbery. Recommended to the clients
by architects Holden & Johnson, and
the interior designer Steve Chase,
Connor joined the team of designers in
their effort to make the pool and garden
area harmonize with the style of the
residence and take full advantage of the
natural setting with the mountains
as a backdrop.

All the boulders and rocks on the site are
natural, since the clients requested that
no artificial rocks be used. The contractor on the job had once been mayor of
Palm Springs, and through him Connor
was able to negotiate an arrangement
with municipal authorities by which he
could use the boulders and rocks removed
in construction of a drainage channel
for the cost of hauling them. While most
of these rocks were used in the rock
garden and the landscaping around the
pool, a select few were lifted into niches
in the pool bondbeam as part of the
walls, placed on ledges, or set on the pool
floor. Additional gunite was blown
around them to create a seal.

The free-form pool is sixty feet at its longest and thirty feet at its widest, with a maximum depth of five feet. Creeping Jenny, pickle rush, sagillaria, and water hyacinths seem resistant to the chemicals in the water, and thrive around the pool.

The garden's two waterfalls help promote a vision of interconnected natural elements. The various waterways of the garden require four separate circulation systems. The vertical waterfall into the pool seems to emanate from the spa, but in fact, the spa and waterfall are on two separate recirculating systems, their mechanisms hidden under a stone bridge over the fall. The cascade waterfall also falls into the pool just a few feet away from the vertical fall. The cascade appears to originate in the stream or the adjoining Koi pond, but it also recirculates the

pool water on its own system. Since the stream is planted with water lilies and other plants that would not tolerate the chlorinated water of the pool, a separate recirculation system is necessary. Because of the size and water volume of the stream, an eleven-foot-long, six-foot-diameter surge tank holds the water when the system is turned off, to prevent flooding.

The pond is an independent ecologically balanced habitat that is not part of any water recirculating system. Here, the Koi dart in and out of the underwater caverns and grottoes thoughtfully provided for them.

Far left: The stepped waterfall between pool and spa is home to a pair of whimsical otter sculptures.

Left: The free-form pool is a pleasing match for the hand-crafted appearance of the residence.

CHAPTER TWO

WORKING

Unless a pool is so far from a residence as to be no more than a distant gleam through the trees, it must have some relationship to the house, and it must be part of the pattern of garden landscaping.

Pools can make definite architectural statements in their relationship to the residence to which they belong. Such pools can be part of the physical structure of the house, or they can be built in close proximity to it, echoing its architectural style and detailing.

The most successful conditions for making the architecture of the pool and the residence complement each other exist when the pool and the house are being built at the same time, but add-on pools can also successfully accomplish this uniform look. Centering the pool on the main line of view to a distant object or point gives a restful integrality to the garden vista, whether consciously recognized or not. Even when the pool is added after the house has been on the property for some time, the garden pattern and pool placement should respect one or more axes, even if only subtly. Some elements of the house architecture can be brought out to the water by incorporating a shade structure or portico, which can be attached to the house or freestanding, depending on the proximity of the pool and house. Paving patterns can also visually link these elements by reaching out from the house to envelop the pool. The shape of the house itself might extend to embrace the pool and entertaining areas in its grid. Most California houses now have living areas at ground level, and the functions of interior spaces flow out onto the patio, where the pool is as much for lounging as it is for swimming.

California's acclaimed landscape architect Tommy Church wrote in his authoritative book *Gardens Are for People:* "The unity of the whole scheme is advanced when the line and material of the house are carried into the garden." And when the garden includes a pool, the same rule must apply.

WITH ARCHITECTURE

Dramatic nighttime lighting makes
the pool a stage, with the city as a
backdrop in the distance.

A sweeping, triangular overhang of concrete with a massive waffle-gridded ceiling
juts over the living room and the pool, producing the effect of a
barrier-free room and pool terrace.

A spectacularly unorthodox residence and swimming pool cling to a slope in the Santa Monica Mountains overlooking West Los Angeles, Beverly Hills, and the Pacific Ocean. Perhaps best described as a contradiction in architecture, the house and pool were built in 1963 from plans by noted architect John Lautner (1911–1994) on a theme of diverse angularity. There are no right angles anywhere, however, except in the rectangular swimming pool.

The residence is a group of wedge-shaped living spaces with angular, yet comfortable furniture, and a canti-levered bedroom, all fashioned in glass, concrete, stainless steel, and wood, with no plaster walls, no handles or knobs, and no visual separation of exterior and interior spaces. A sweeping, peaked triangular overhang of concrete with a massive waffle-gridded ceiling juts, apparently unsupported, over the living room and the pool, producing the effect of a barrier-free room and pool terrace. Lautner embedded 750 inverted water tumblers in the soaring waffled ceiling as a firmament of miniature skylights, through which the sunlight pours in beacons, vying with the reflections from the pool.

When the current resident, real-estate developer James Goldstein, bought the house in 1972, both the house and the pool were, in Goldstein's own words, "in horrendous condition." The previous owners had not understood Lautner's vision. But Goldstein saw magnificent possibilities, and he contacted Lautner.

As it was originally designed in 1963,
there was only a forced-air curtain between
the house and pool.

The many lights in the overhang are reflected in the pool, as if imitating the lights of the city spread out below.

Together they renovated the residence and pool, restoring and enhancing the original Lautner design, including installing a gutter detail that raised the water level of the pool to lie flush with the deck and appear like a sheet of glass seemingly extending into space. Goldstein and Lautner worked together until Lautner's death in 1994.

When the house was first built, Michigan-born Lautner, like many other California transplants, believed that California living could be outdoors all year round, and he provided only a curtain of forced air as a barrier between the living room and the pool area. This feature was replaced with a row of windows by a subsequent owner. Lautner and Goldstein in turn created an invisible wall of huge, half-inch-thick glass panels, which preserves the integrality of the living space and pool area. This effect is reinforced by the fact that floor surfaces and pool decking are now consistent— a pebbled, natural-colored concrete. The pool itself is of the same aggregate, and when filled with water, Goldstein says, it looks like the shallow waters of a tropical sea.

The forty-by-sixteen-foot pool is kept warm by radiant heat from hot water pipes embedded in the concrete. The pool water recirculates from a holding tank so big that it had to be lifted by helicopter and positioned under the cantilevered bedroom in the slope on which the house is built. As in most sophisticated pool systems, all functions such as heating, filtering, and lighting can be controlled from a central panel.

The house has one particularly unusual feature—in the bedroom, observation windows face into the pool underwater. "The purpose of architecture," wrote Lautner shortly before his death, "is to improve human life; create timeless, free, joyous spaces!" The Goldstein residence and swimming pool exuberantly follow that credo.

"The line of a spline of limestone begins at the motor court near the street and continues through the entry garden, the house itself, across the pool, and over the spa . . . uniting the internal and external elements of the house."

The monumental geometry of the house is picked up in the pool area in outdoor "rooms" defined by limestone and lawn.

The thoroughly contemporary house and swimming pool designed by architect Don Hensman of Buff, Smith & Hensman and built in Brentwood in 1988, is a prime example of how a pool and a residence can become a unified architectural form. The firm describes the theme element of the project in this way: "The line of a spline of limestone begins at the motor court near the street and continues through the entry garden, the house itself, across the pool, and over the spa, terminating at a sculptural wall at the property's east side, thus uniting the internal and external elements of the house."

This axis walkway that stretches like a raised fashion runway through the house, is made with twenty-four-inch limestone squares running six feet wide and 130 feet long, until it descends to the pool level. Two steps down on either side, it is bordered by the rooms of the residence as well as outdoor living spaces, making it difficult to determine if a given space is an exterior space that is furnished, or an interior space that is landscaped. Architect Hensman adds: "The use of frameless glass adds to the illusion of no separation between different living spaces. The mitered corners of the glass tend to exaggerate the illusion of openness."

The limestone paving continues around
the forty-two-by-twelve-foot rectangular
swimming pool to form the decking
and edging, and sweeps back to surround
the square spa located on the far side of
the pool. The narrow spill channel that
runs from the spa to the pool extends
beyond the spa to a sculpture wall in
which a vertical gap echoes the horizontal

The limestone walkway to the pool (p. 54) is continued in negative space on the opposite side: a narrow spill channel connects to the spa, then to a gap in the wall beyond.

channel and accentuates the sense of the axis that unifies the entire living space. The small waterfall into the pool recirculates the spa water.

The pool is plastered green with green tiles at the water's edge, and is gas heated. Designed to be safe for children, it is only three feet deep at each end, and four feet in the middle, ideal for both playing and swimming.

Landscape architect Garret Carlson underscored the classic simplicity of the pool area by placing large pottery urns bursting with flowers in strategic spots, and furthered the illusion of joined interior and exterior spaces by designing precise, squared patches of lawn set into the limestone paving like large green rugs.

WORKING WITH ARCHITECTURE: STONERIDGE

An overhang of lodge-pole pine and hand-hewn beams is supported
by stuccoed columns that echo the color and style of the house,
tying pool, overhang, and house together.

The building materials of the pool, and its columnar forms, are consistent in this design, presenting a unified outdoor space.

Inspired by a southwestern-style house with terra-cotta-colored walls built in 1984 in Bel Air's Stoneridge Estates, Galper/Baldon Associates of Venice, California designed a pool and patio to accentuate the pueblo feeling of the home. To complement the house, which was built simultaneously with the pool, the firm designed an assertive overhang of rustic lodge-pole pine and hand-hewn beams, supported by stuccoed columns that echo the color and style of the house, tying pool, overhang, and house together. The raised bondbeam edge of the pool perimeter acts as seating, its short pillars echoing the shape of the bases of the columns.

The L-shaped pool is forty by twelve and one-half feet with a nine-by-eighteen-foot offset that holds a spa and entry steps. The offset section is edged in forest green tiles to match the tile-lined inside edge of the pool. The tiles are hard bodied and highly glazed to discourage the formation of algae.

In this case, the spa is part of the pool, but is separated from it by an underwater dam that allows circulation and heating of pool and spa water at the same time. The spa water can then be super-heated with the touch of a button before use.

Often, spas are separate from the pool and are kept hot enough for use at any time. These are usually covered to retain the heat and retard evaporation. Spas of all types are increasingly seen in California since the invention by Candido Jacuzzi (1903–1986) of air jet injection for water massage, and the recognition of its pleasurable therapeutic value. Since the innovation by Galper/Baldon Associates of contoured underwater seating, patented in 1973 by Hydro-Spa, the once straight-sided prefabricated spas with flat benches are now almost all made with ergonomic contours, and come in all sizes. Once made of fiberglass, most prefabricated spas today are made of acrylic.

Just as pools are designed in myriad styles—whether natural, highly ornamented, indoors, or out—spas can also be designed to satisfy almost any requirement. The patio and pool area at Stoneridge is just one example of a successful coordination of spa and pool, landscaping, and architecture.

At the spectacular residence and pool of housing developers Diane and Jim Clarke in La Jolla,
built directly on the ocean shore, it is difficult to discern where the house ends
and the pool begins.

At the spectacular residence and pool of housing developers Diane and Jim Clarke in La Jolla, built directly on the ocean shore, it is difficult to discern where the house ends and the pool begins. The whole pool complex is an intriguing maze of steps, decks, and pools fully integrated with the impressive residence.

The cluster of pools consists of a lap pool with a spur at each end and a weir and waterfall, a diving pool, and a spa. The architect, Ken Ronchetti, is an award-winning designer of gardens and pools, and he designed the house and pools to be integral parts of each other, sharing architectural lines, building materials, and structure. Ronchetti calls the multifaceted pool "a water sculpture to enhance the form of the house as a transition to the ocean and as an adventure in swimming."

In 1990 when the Clarkes bought the land on which to build their new home, there was already a partially demolished house and an empty pool on the property. Because of the existing pool, part of which they were able to reuse, the Clarkes could plan their new pool where they wanted it, rather than adjusting their plans to new coastal restrictions requiring a twenty-five-foot setback. In this way, they were able to realize their dream of a house and pool directly on the ocean shore.

The residence stands on a twenty-five-foot cliff over a small sandy beach below that is so narrow it cannot be seen from the house, and it appears as if the house and pool stand directly at the water's edge. There is a striking view from the mid-level living room across the pools to the ocean surf below. To heighten the illusion of openness, the glass wall that runs the length of the room is dropped six inches below floor level so that no anchoring edge can be seen.

Seven feet below the level of the living room is the fifty-five-by-nine-foot lap pool. A seven-foot weir on one edge of it spills water ten feet down, where it lands in the diving pool after coursing under a bridge with inlaid glass panels that leads to a spa designed in the shape of a hiero-glyphic eye. A flight of stairs in the waterfall well leads to the diving pool, where one can dive from the bridge or from different levels on the grand staircase opposite the spa.

All construction materials were chosen for their ability to resist the corrosive effects of the salt water climate.

The galvanized metal of the handrails is painted with powder coating and the French limestone decking is periodically treated with a penetrating sealer. There is no wood trim.

The controls for all the equipment— gas heaters, recirculating and filtering systems, lighting, waterfall, air injection, and even the background music— are located under the house, and are either automatic or part of an intricate, computer controlled low-voltage system. These controls can also be adjusted from several locations in the house, from the spa area, and even from the car.

In spite of the intricacy of their pool, the ocean is very much part of the lives of Diane and Jim Clarke. At high tide the surf thundering against the cliff can soar above the cliff top. Seaweed often festoons the pool security fence on the edge, and the ocean occasionally leaves the gift of a large fish deposited on the turf.

Multiple pools offer various options: swim laps in the lap pool, descend into the waterfall well, relax in the spa, or dive from the bridge or the stairs.

The formal swimming pool is set in a structured setting
strongly influenced by Tuscan and Venetian garden styles.

The formal pool is parallel to the house, with a vast lawn and rose parterres connecting them.

The formal swimming pool and Italian-style villa owned by Matthew White and Thomas Schumacher symmetrically complement each other in a balanced setting strongly influenced by Tuscan and Venetian garden styles. The estate was built in this Los Angeles County community in 1924 by the father-and-son architectural firm of Weston & Weston on a city lot of more than an acre. White and Schumacher are both active in neighboring Pasadena's civic affairs, and they use the lovely villa and elegant pool area to stage fund-raisers and benefits, official ceremonies, and other forms of entertainment.

The formal architectural landscaping of the grounds is designed on east/west and north/south axes. From the east, centered on a pair of imposing French doors in the villa, an expanse of well-manicured lawn flanked by flourishing parterre rose gardens sweeps down to a broad flight of four steps to the pool level. Across the pool is a small semi-circular observation platform with a view over a rose garden four steps below. Here are three fountains, one of which anchors the west end of the axis. The others are placed at the north and at the south end of the garden with a flight of steps and a U-shaped landing around each one, connecting the pool and west garden levels. The three fountains are connected by narrow channels of water.

The pool is anchored on one end by a spa,
and on the other by an Italian-style pool house
(not shown).

Putti at either end of the pool maintain
the classical tone of the grounds while adding
a playful note to the formal estate.

The pool itself is built on the north/south axis, with a pool house at the south end and a raised spa at the north end. The pool is a classic rectangle thirty-six feet long and fourteen feet wide. Both the pool and the spa are ringed in low, neatly trimmed privet hedges that echo the hedges enclosing the rose parterres. A low privet hedge also sets apart the lower west garden and its fountains. The pool is plastered black with a French limestone decking and pool edge; below the lip it is ringed with tiles. The pool area is surrounded by tall trees including eucalyptus, crepe myrtle, and palms, whose reflections shimmer and sparkle in the water at night when the trees are lit with floodlights. On a raised platform at each end of the pool stands a bronze putti, a classical touch of whimsy in these neat, formal gardens.

In 1970 the lap pool made its appearance in California, emerging to coincide with a heightened interest in physical fitness, and became popular almost instantly. Credited to Cleo Baldon, design director of the Venice, California-based landscape architecture firm Galper/Baldon Associates, the lap pool is designed for exercise.

According to Baldon, it was inspired by the long, narrow irrigation ditches of her apple-country childhood, in which her mother had forbidden her to swim.

Long and narrow, the lap pool gives the swimmer an opportunity to swim lap after lap of the pool unencumbered, and because of its narrowness this pool often fits where pools of more conventional sizes will not. A minimum forty-foot length is adequate for serious swimming, and the swimmer will have a comfortable swimming stroke in a pool that is only eight or nine feet wide. A depth of three feet at the shallow end, four feet in the middle, and five feet for easy standing in the deep end is ideal. Often the lap pool has a leg at the shallow end where children can play, and where the access steps are located.

The construction, maintenance, and heating of this pool is the same as for other pools. The lap pool, however, can be equipped with a machine that creates a strong, steady artificial current, so the swimmer can swim in place against a continuous flow of water, without forward motion or the need to turn at the end of the pool.

Even though the lap pool is more functional than other pools, it can be just as luxuriously constructed and land-scaped as its larger counterparts, and can provide a relatively small garden with a beautiful and useful water element.

CHAPTER THREE

THE LAP POOL

THE LAP POOL: HOLLYWOOD

The house is located deep in a hairpin turn, and there seemed to be
no space whatsoever to accommodate a pool.

Abundant planting, an arbor,
and lattices turn the pool area into an
outdoor room where birds and squirrels are
at home on the wooden beams overhead.

In the tip of a hairpin turn on a winding
street just north of Sunset Boulevard
in Hollywood stands a two-story,
Spanish-style house almost hidden by
trees and verdant shrubbery. The house
was built in 1924 when the Hollywood
Hills were still resort land, and it now
belongs to the authors, Cleo Baldon
Melchior and Ib Melchior.

We lived in this house for twenty years
before we decided in 1987 that we wanted
a swimming pool. Since the house is
located deep in the hairpin turn, however,
there seemed to be no space whatsoever
to accommodate a pool. In the tip of the
turn, just north of the house, there was a
small patio surrounded by a stand of
bamboo. The area was about eighty-five
feet long and twenty-two feet wide,
tapering at each end near the road. This
was the only place available.

Because of the constrictive site, a lap
pool was the only choice. The patio was
removed, and a pool forty by eight feet
with a depth ranging from three to six
and one-half feet was built. At one end on
a small incline is a rock garden covered
with fern and baby-tear moss, and a stand
of clivia providing color. A dry streambed
of pebbles leads into a fish pond stocked
with goldfish and water lilies. Two
small waterfalls splash into the pond,
circulating and aerating its water. One
waterfall seems to come from the adjoining swimming pool, a deliberate illusion
that ties the water elements together.
At the opposite end of the pool, a built-in
stone lounge for two with a terry-cloth-

On the near end of the pool,
a waterfall spills into the fish pond,
and at the far end are the access
steps and a padded stone
bench for lounging.

covered pad offers a comfortable rest for
the swimmer after exercising.

The pool and the entire pool area are constructed of Idaho quartz. The pool edge
bordering the patio is raised fourteen
inches above the ground to provide forty

feet of seating. A protrusion forms a table for leisurely dining. The far edge of the pool is raised one foot further above the water line to contain *Podocarpus henkelii*, asparagus ferns, and star jasmine which are allowed to bush out over the water. On this far edge a lattice arbor forms a niche framing a beautiful, eight-foot-tall

Italian bronze and marble fountain that serves as a drinking fountain for doves and blue jays. The overhang of wooden beams, its pillars resting on the raised edge of the pool, ties the water to the house, which is only eight feet away with a glass wall that leaves it open to the enchanting outdoor room.

The children's pool overlooks
the lap pool, and water spills from one
to the other over a weir edge.

THE LAP POOL: THE MONTALBAN POOL

Ricardo Legorreta designed this striking house and two pools in the
Mexican-inspired style typical of his work.

Above: Georgiana Montalban, who planned the pool's color scheme, enjoys the soothing splash of water from the two fountains and the weir.

Right: The massive forms that are a Legorreta signature enclose and shelter the children's swimming area, making it part of the house while still allowing a view out over the neighborhood.

This architecturally striking pool in the Doheny region of Los Angeles is really two pools. The property is owned by Ricardo Montalban—the movie star who has appeared in more than fifty motion pictures including *The Reluctant Saint, The Singing Nun,* and *A Life in the Balance,* and who played the mysterious host of Fantasy Island—and his wife Georgiana, an interior designer who selected the pleasing complementary color scheme of the house and pool.

Ricardo Legorreta designed both the house and the pools in the Mexican-inspired style typical of his work. His design incorporates three primary elements from Mexican culture: walls, water, and earth colors.

The Montalbans wanted a pool for swimming, in which children could also play safely. Raised about three feet above the patio level between a wall of the house and a tall ornamental wall, Legorreta placed a twenty-by-twenty-foot pool that is only three feet deep for the children. Water from this pool spills over a weir into a second pool below, a lap pool sixty feet long by ten feet wide and four and one-half feet deep, where the Montalbans can swim undisturbed. Legorreta controls spacial perception on this wide-open patio with the blue wall and overhead that partially enclose the children's swimming area and guide the eye to the echoing blue wall at the far end of the lap pool. Each of these two walls contains a remote-controlled fount, separate from the pool recirculation system.

The areas between house and pool are perfect for entertaining, with a view of the hills, across the city to the ocean, and to Catalina Island beyond.

THE LAP POOL: MALIBU COLONY

The pool area is open to the sand and ocean, but is protected by a glass buffer wall
or windscreen that is barely noticeable against the background of water and sky.

Carefully placed barriers and plantings shield the patio and pool from the adjoining properties, and direct the eye to the ocean.

Building lots along the Malibu Beach are long and narrow and pointed toward the beach, to give water access to as many residents as possible. The houses are close together, some built right at the water's edge and supported by piles that are often battered by the surf at high tide. Others are built farther back from the water with a raised platform deck and sometimes a swimming pool between the house and the ocean. Just such a residence, covered with gray clapboard and trimmed in white like a New England beach cottage, was designed and built on speculation by architects Ron Goldman and Bob Firth.

The raised platform on which the house and pool are built is paved with Bouquet Canyon flagstones that begin with the entry court at the street, run through the ground floor of the house, and form the deck around the pool. The Bouquet Canyon flag is a relatively hard and corrosion-resistant stone that can dip into the water of the pool without deterioration, therefore no pool tile edging is necessary. The pool area is open to the sand and ocean, but is protected by a glass buffer wall or windscreen that is barely noticeable against the background of water and sky.

The lap pool is twenty-nine feet long and ten feet wide, with a tri-level deck. From the house, French doors lead to a patio area at the same level, from which the view to the ocean passes over the heads of the crowds on the beach, directly connecting the viewer with the sea. The pool on this end is above ground level, providing seating and acting as a safety barrier in the close space. Two steps up from the patio, at water level, there is also a seven-by-five-foot spa, and one further step up is a teak sun deck and observation point, a more public spot from which to survey the beach scene.

The walls on either side of the property, of teak-wood boards in a horizontal configuration, define the property's boundaries while respecting the materials and colors of the house, and guiding the eye down the deck toward the sea. This minimizes awareness of the closely adjoining lots, and the myoporum or salt bushes along the walls on each side soften the feeling of containment and provide a further measure of privacy on this crowded stretch of beach.

This measured combination of a natural pool and a more conventional one
creates a harmonious and pleasing landscape.

The shape of the spa mirrors that
of the pool entry steps; the two are linked
by a narrow channel.

The home of Carol Soucek King and
Richard King, built in 1979, is located in
an arroyo in Pasadena, and because of this
remains in shadow longer in the morning
and becomes shaded earlier in the evening
than houses built on higher ground.
The forty-by-twelve-foot lap pool, built
at the same time as the residence, is therefore white with a white tile border, and
the deck surrounding it and forming
a spacious terrace at one end consists of
beige, poured-in-place pebble aggregate.
Because of these features, the pool and
the area around it are bright and cheerful.
A dark-colored pool would have been
more economical by retaining heat
efficiently, but the Kings feel that the
brightness their pool lends to the property
is well worth the extra cost of maintenance and heating. By the same token
they have opted not to use a heat-saving
cover over the pool, since they want to
enjoy its serenity and beauty around the
clock. The pool's four-foot depth, however, helps make heating less costly.

The pool and garden comprise an elaborate sculpture, with different paving materials defining zones, and rocks and plantings placed as focal points. Even the distant highway overpass contributes to the composition.

Designed by architects Buff, Smith & Hensman, this measured combination of a natural pool and a more conventional one creates a harmonious and pleasing landscape. Various deck materials are used—the pebble aggregate shares space with natural, grouted paving stones and areas of loose rounded gravel spread over heavy plastic sheets to keep the weeds from sprouting among the pebbles. Large, tumbled river boulders are placed to define viewpoints on the landscape. Stone steps alternate with railroad-tie risers and planked walkways, and large natural stepping stones lead to the house.

A spa is connected to the pool by a narrow channel, which visually links the shape of the spa with that of the entry steps across the pool, and the forms of the house beyond. The area is planted with isles of green ground cover such as mondo grass, ivy, and fountain grass, and with low shrubbery, including oleanders, azaleas, and juniper. The landscape is influenced by the tailored Japanese gardens of Kyoto and Osaka, and gives way to a wild area beyond the tended garden.

Tall trees such as acacias, eucalyptuses, and native California oaks, as well as various bushes, surround the entire garden, ensuring privacy and making the spot ideal for outdoor gatherings with family and friends.

Aside from the landscaped boulder and rock edge of the natural residential swimming pool, there are two principal types of edging: the flush or level edge is virtually flush with the surrounding deck, and the surface of the water is a mere few inches below; the raised edge is at seating height above deck level, with the water level raised correspondingly.

The edge or rim of the pool is built on the gunite bondbeam, capping it. Flush edges can be tiled or paved with flagstones or other flat stones, or sculpted in concrete, with a lip overhanging the pool by a couple of inches. An alternative to this poured-in-place coping is a precast concrete coping that can be set into a grout bed.

The raised edge can provide convenient seating all around the pool, or a platform on which to place flower pots or statuary. The pool deck can be made of various materials—flagstones, concrete, tiles, bricks, patio blocks, redwood, lawn, mixed aggregate, or even outdoor carpeting.

In the eighties in California a spectacular innovation came into use—that of lowering a part of the pool rim to just below the water's surface, thus creating a fall of water out of the pool and into a receiving channel below, to be recirculated into the pool. This idea is particularly effective on hillsides where there is no close background on the dropped side of the pool and the water appears to flow into the sky; or on a beach, where the pool and the ocean appear almost as one.

In the nineties this design has come to be known as the infinity edge; it can range from a couple of feet in length to a couple of dozen feet, or the full length of the pool. The water can plunge as far as twenty feet. A successful smooth weir must have an absolutely level edge for the water to flow over. As an alternative to the smooth weir, a slightly turbulent flow can be achieved by embedding gravel or small stones in the weir edge, thus creating a different look, more like a waterfall.

Access to the pool can be handled in various ways. Usually a series of steps at the shallow end, part of the design and construction of the pool, leads into the water. Or a "beach access," a gradual slope made of the same material as the deck or the pool, can lead into the water. To reach a depth of three feet, an access ramp of twenty-one feet is required, or seven feet of ramp to every foot of depth.

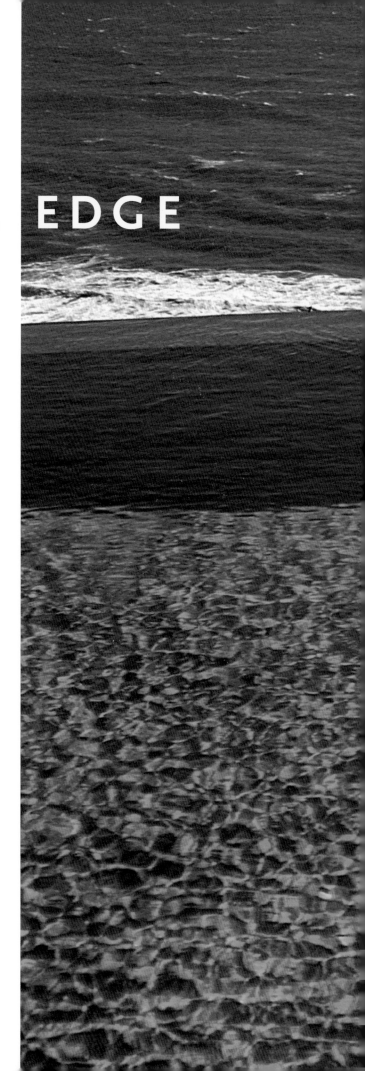

CHAPTER FOUR

THE POOL EDGE

Earlier pools may have ladders, generally
made of stainless steel with three or four
stainless steel or plastic treads. The handrails are embedded in the concrete or
gunite as the pool is poured.

The overflow system of the pool forms
part of the edge as well. In older pools
a scum gutter and overflow system below
the lip of the pool was necessary, but the
improvement of pool circulation and
filtering systems today makes a simple
overflow pipe at water level sufficient.
These technical details affect the appearance of the pool to some small extent,
but a successful pool edge is ultimately
the product of an innovative design that
complements the style of nearby architecture, and fulfills the wishes of
the owners.

Two columns are reflected across the mirror-like surface of the
pool, tying house and pool together.

The extremely smooth flow of water over the weir prompts visitors to touch it to see if it really is wet.

On a hilltop in the Encino hills lies a swimming pool with a dramatic configuration. Designed by Cleo Baldon of Galper/Baldon Associates, the pool is directly connected both physically and visually with the residence, a two-story contemporary house designed by architect Randy Washington. The pool is placed on a precise axis that runs from the center of the house facade to the tip of the rise on which the property is located, splitting the pool in identical halves.

The forty-by-sixteen-foot rectangular pool is connected with the house by an area of decking running the length of the pool. Two narrow inlets reach back from the pool toward the house like twelve-foot hinges, allowing two columns that support a balcony of the residential structure to be footed in the water and reflect their full height across the mirror-like surface of the pool. This architectural feature is possible because the house and the pool were constructed at the same time. The inlets can be crossed by two stepping stone pedestals placed in the water.

The symmetrical design of house and pool enhances their monumental formality.

The pool is plastered black and edge-tiled with glazed black tiles. The three underwater steps that run the full length of the pool at the inside decking are also covered with black tiles, as are the weir edge and outside wall. Eight broad stripes of beige tiles cross the treads of the steps and pick up again on the twenty-two-inch weir bondbeam and the outside wall, emphasizing the unusual width of the weir. These stripes continue the paths of the columns reflected in the water, tying house and pool together, as if with ribbon. The water that gently flows over the weir and down the side of the pool is so smooth and even, with nary a ripple to betray it, that visitors invariably touch it to see if it really is wet. Below, the water is collected in a trough with a small over-flow pond, to be recirculated to the pool. This pond and a black-plastered and -tiled spa are located six steps below the upper terrace, and are reached by short flights of steps on either side of the pool. The decking and steps are paved with French limestone pavers.

The formal pool area is surrounded by careful landscaping including carissa and privet hedges, sycamores, and pine trees that frame the view from the living room of the residence, over the serene weir of the swimming pool to the rolling hills and valleys of the Santa Monica Mountains.

The half-moon-shaped pool extends from the precipitous slope,
its depth gradually increasing from the steps to the weir.

The perfect surface of the water looks like a sheet of glass, and reflects everything on its edge.

Evoking the colonnaded splendor of the ancient pools at Hadrian's Villa outside Rome, this pool in the hills of Montecito offers a thirty-foot curved infinity edge and a spectacular view of the wooded slopes below, and the Pacific Ocean and Channel Islands in the far distance. The pool belongs to architectural designer Robert Woolf, who coveted the estate, sans pool, ever since he first saw it in the mid-1950s. It was not until 1995, however, that Woolf became the owner of the Italian-style villa built in 1918 by the McGann family.

He immediately set out to renovate and remodel the estate, and particularly to build a swimming pool. The existing pool at the estate was a rather small indoor pool in a pool house on the slope below the main residence. Woolf filled in the pool and converted the pool house to a cabana, enclosed on three sides. Canvas curtains hang in the open side of the cabana, which faces the slope on which Woolf constructed a sixty-four-by-thirty-three-foot limestone terrace with planted parterres, accessed by two flights of stairs leading down from the villa. At the end of this terrace Woolf built his fantasy pool.

In contrast to the serene arc of water
above (p. 90), the rough verde slate surface
of the weir makes the water splash
noisily into the basin below.

The pool and garden, with their classical references, are perfectly in keeping with the grandeur of the original Italian-style villa.

Designed in the shape of an extended half-moon, the pool is forty feet long on the straight edge, where four steps running its entire length lead into the water from the terrace. Extending from the precipitous slope, the depth of this carefully engineered pool gradually increases from the steps to the weir, where it is shoulder-deep. Flanking the weir are two pairs of ancient stone columns from Italy that reach formally toward the sky.

The weir is covered with rough verde slate and the plaster of the pool is colored to match. The water brims unevenly over the weir and runs turbulently down an

irregularly surfaced, seventeen-foot wall to a collection and recirculation basin below that hugs the curvature of the pool and is bordered by beds planted with low hedges. From here a lawn extends down the slope to an ornamental wall and fountain at the far end.

An additional feature of this charming property is a recently renovated funicular, which was originally constructed in the 1960s. Three hundred feet long, it runs to a picnic area by a creek below.

The effects of the infinity edge are here
displayed to perfection.

THE POOL EDGE: A POOL ON MALIBU BEACH

On a seventy-five-foot bluff overlooking the Pacific Ocean, the water from the pool
smoothly and evenly brims over a crescent-shaped wall facing the ocean and
cascades into a reservoir below.

Left: The tip of the pool would make an inconvenient corner for lap-swimming; it is made into a raised sculptural element with a small weir of its own.

Above: From the patio, there is little evidence of the other houses on the hillside.

In 1985 when Canadian pool designer Barry Beer moved his company, Beer & Associates, from Canada to California, he expected his business to boom—and it did!

Beer thinks of a pool as a large sculpture which must blend with its surroundings and architecturally complement the home. To this end, he uses simple lines and a dramatic style to create his elegant designs, such as his pool for clients in Malibu in 1990. He calls it his infinity pool: on a seventy-five-foot bluff overlooking the Pacific Ocean, the water from the pool smoothly and evenly brims over a crescent-shaped wall facing the ocean

and cascades into a reservoir below for re-circulation. The slight turbulence created when the pool filter system is operating results in a water surface similar to the waves on the ocean beyond. The slate-colored spillway edge and pool plaster allow the water to echo the ever-changing color of the Pacific. From the raised deck made of sand-textured French limestone that surrounds three sides of the fifty-two-foot-long pool, or viewed from indoors through a continuous wall of doors and windows, the pool does seem to merge with the ocean beyond; the line of demarcation is all but invisible.

Designed not only for swimming, the pool is also part of California outdoor living. With a southerly exposure, the sun—moving along the length of the pool—provides daylong light and warmth for lounging and entertaining at poolside. An elevated plinth twelve by twelve feet square at the northwest end of the pool holds a fireplace and a spa, from which the view of both pool and ocean can be enjoyed in sybaritic comfort.

"The pool and the spillway draw the Pacific's edge
closer...in a manner which interacts but never interferes
with the natural coastline." —*Barry Beer*

Landscape architect June King designed an eye-catching triangular pool
that complements the lines of the residence.

The shapes of the pool and spa complement each other, their lines receding toward the horizon.

In Sonoma, just north of San Francisco, is an unusual triangular pool. Robert Zinkham, the residential architect, felt that each side of the pool should parallel a wing of the house, and landscape architect June King embraced the idea and designed an eye-catching triangular pool that complements the lines of the residence.

The length of the black-plastered pool at the hypotenuse is forty-one feet; the longer of the remaining sides is thirty-four feet; and the shortest side, which is truncated, is twenty-four feet long. The short side has a ten-foot weir that spills into a holding tank below. Access to the pool is provided by steps situated in the right angle and sheltered by a small promontory that juts into the water. The edge of the pool and the deck surrounding it is paved with hand-cut, -shaped, and -smoothed flagstones of uniform color.

Water enters the pool from a rockscaped knoll about forty feet away, located near a cabana and an arbor. The water bubbles up from the ground like a natural spring, cascades over a small waterfall and splashes through a channel of rocks and boulders from local quarries, then dips under the flagstone decking and gently flows into the pool. The water then spills over the weir at the far end and into the holding tank, from which it is recirculated.

Water from the source on a rocky knoll
flows beneath the flagstones, which offer glimpses
through a series of "windows."

Water in this hilly area of Sonoma is provided by a series of wells, and must be softened before use, which limits the household supply. In order to fill the pool before the plaster dried, the owner was forced to have the large volume of water brought to the site by truck. Evaporation and other water loss can, however, be made up from the household supply. Since natural gas is also unavailable, the pool is heated with propane. The spa on the edge of the pool has its own heating and filtering system and is kept hot year-round.

The pool was finished in 1985, but a few years later a manzanita that had been planted on the knoll at the water source died. King found a suitable replacement, and—after excavating part of the knoll and dismantling part of the arbor nearby to enable a crane to set the fourteen-foot-tall successor in its place—today a Scotch pine showing years of healthy growth towers over the knoll and the triangular pool below.

Part of the design of a pool is often the reflections it catches at its edge—here, a planting of purple *Echium fastuosum* and the native oaks beyond the weir.

CHAPTER FIVE

THE LANGUAGE OF

Ever since prehistoric clans painted animals and traced finger-splayed hands
on cave walls, the human desire to adorn our surroundings has been evident, and through the ages
the development of swimming pools has revealed them to be
a focal point for such ornamentation.

Ancient natatoria of the Persian, Egyptian, Moorish, and Byzantine cultures were elaborately ornamented with intricately designed, multi-colored mosaics, tiled surfaces, carved columns, and statuary in niches and alcoves.

In contrast to the Greek pools, which were more like gymnasiums, the Roman pools were lavishly ornamented. The frigidarium (outdoor swimming pool) of Caracalla in Rome (211–17 CE) was surrounded by marble columns crowned by statues. The columns were set in the water in such a way that their complete images were reflected on its surface. The Roman tepidarium (an indoor pool) featured richly ornamented ceilings, arches, and walls. Many of the private villas of Rome had swimming baths in peristyled courtyards with rich frescoes and mosaic paving. A marine mosaic in the Baths of Neptune in Ostia, the port of Rome, depicts Neptune and his chariot drawn by four horses and surrounded by swimmers and sea creatures. The House

of Papyri excavated in Pompeii had a pool six by sixty-six meters (about 20 by 216 feet) surrounded by a peristyle of sixty-five columns and works of art, culminating in a life-sized statue of a sleeping faun reflected in the water. This villa and pool have been reconstructed at the J. Paul Getty Museum in Malibu—the garden and the pool under the supervision of noted landscape architect Emmet Wemple.

There are three principal ways in which to embellish a pool: by adorning the pool itself with tiles, mosaics, fountains, and waterfalls; by enhancing the surroundings with pavilions, columns, statues, and sculptures; and by accessorizing the area with potted plants and rockscapes, flowers and trees that reflect in the water, and other eye-catching natural accoutrements.

ORNAMENT

Ornament can be so exuberant that the
pool itself is of relatively minor importance, such as in the color-splashed oasis
of Tony Duquette—or a measured
touch of sophisticated tile work can be
used to transform just one part of the
outdoor area, such as the Moorish fountain in Santa Barbara. Opulent or
understated, ornament is the key to the
setting and mood of every pool.

THE LANGUAGE OF ORNAMENT: THE DUQUETTE POOL

Behind a tall, green lattice wall on a small hillside street in Beverly Hills,
cradled in a green tropical jungle, lies a swimming pool and environment
of unequaled originality, the product of a taste for the exotic
and a splash of vivid imagination.

Lush plants and brightly painted wood suggest a Far Eastern temple, and attest to the success of Tony Duquette's stage design.

Built in 1989, the thirty-by-fifteen-foot rectangular pool is enclosed on two sides by double-level balconies and a lattice overhang extending from the house, all in brightly painted, carved wood. On the other two sides of the pool are patios and gardens. Bursting with lush plants and flowers including bird's nest ferns, spider plants, ivy, impatiens, and azaleas, it is a constantly changing cloister of flora. In this riot of greenery, picturesque pagodas and pavilions, exotic sculptures, large planted jars and urns, and intricate peacock fans and sunbursts lend a foreign mystique. The dark water of the black-plastered pool adds to the magical aura—and helps keep the gas-heated pool warm. The rim is edged in dark, blue tiles and the deck is also dark, due to black pigment added to the concrete at pouring. The shimmering white medallions with sunburst designs set with tiles in the bottom of the dark pool are, according to the owner, ancient symbols for power. The close proximity to the water of the plants and the wooden tiers insures strong, clear reflections on the pool. The lavishly carved bridge at one end of the pool was added at a later stage of the constantly evolving garden design.

The owner of this vibrant pool is Tony Duquette, the internationally renowned

Above: Fanciful sculptures populate the garden, from which a short staircase leads to the gallery above the pool.

Right: The white medallions, ancient symbols of power on the bottom of the pool, interact with the reflections of sunburst shapes and peacock tails from the temple-shaped bridge at the end of the pool.

artist and designer whose work has influenced entire fields of creativity. He designed the sets for many motion pictures, including *The Ziegfeld Follies* (1946), and for Broadway plays such as *Kismet* (1953). He won a Tony for the costuming of the original Broadway production of *Camelot* (1958) and was honored with a one-man exhibition of his work at the Louvre in 1952. He counts a host of luminaries, including Mary Pickford, the Duke and Duchess of Windsor, J. Paul Getty, and Sharon Stone, among his clients, for whom he has designed interiors, jewelry, sculpture, and other decorations, but Duquette is never more exuberant than when he designs for himself. He and his late wife and partner, Elizabeth—whom he and everyone else affectionately called Beegle—created a world all their own.

This hillside patio and pool with a multi-tiered, richly ornamented fountain are buffered
from the noise of a nearby highway by the large house that shelters the outdoor living area,
both built in 1991 by the architectural firm Sharp, Mahan & Lenny.

The shape of the fountainhead echoes the Moorish-Spanish-style windows of the house.

This hillside patio and pool with a multi-tiered, richly ornamented fountain are buffered from the noise of a nearby highway by the large house that shelters the outdoor living area, both built in 1991 by the architectural firm Sharp, Mahan & Lenny. The house and pool are in the Moorish-Spanish style of much of the architecture in Santa Barbara. The roof tiles on the house are copied from old models—thick, barreled tiles from a time when tile makers shaped the clay on their thigh. The balustrade on the wall above the fountain and along one side of the forty-by-fourteen-foot pool is Piñon Contrera stone, hand carved in Mexico. The tiles of the fountain were made from patterns developed in the 1920s. The owners had to wait two years for the ornamental jardinieres which were to be placed on the fountain. They were being made locally, also from old patterns, but just as they were about to be installed, the San Fernando earthquake of January 1994 struck. The jardinieres were broken, and the owners had to wait another six months for delivery.

The fountain is always running and its pleasant white noise masks the residual sounds of traffic on the highway. On the top tier of the fountain is a spa which receives the fountain stream and overflows down the steps into the pool. The pool is solar heated using lines embedded in the concrete, which absorbs the heat of the sun and heats the water recirculating through the lines. A gas heater supplies additional heat when needed, and a computer in the house indicates the proportions of solar heat and gas heat used at all times. The spa shares the pool's heating and filtering system, but can also be heated separately, reaching 103 degrees within a few minutes. Its relaxing environment is made only more peaceful by the view over a green golf course to the mature trees of an early ranch and the ocean in the distance.

Water spills from the fountain into the spa, then down the spa steps into the pool.

The stark outlining and symmetry of the pool's basic structure is softened by the oriental jars
and urns that line the edges and introduce fine detail and eye-catching color,
yet maintain the balance of the overall scheme.

Color, reflection, pattern, and the classic principles of garden design each play a subtle part in the success of this pool.

This thirty-by-ten-foot swimming pool on a hillside street in the Outpost, an early subdivision of Los Angeles, lies on the spot where the original 1936 building plans called for a rose garden—a trivial fact discovered by an odd coincidence.

On their way to a dinner party in the mid-1980s, interior designer Hutton Wilkinson and his wife Ruth happened to drive by an old, rundown house and overgrown yard that looked familiar. When Wilkinson realized that the house had been built in 1936 by his father's and grandfather's architectural firm, it took only brief deliberation before the couple decided to buy it. They learned that the original clients and owners of the house had sold it in 1952 and it had stood empty ever since. Within a year they had restored the house and garden and built the pool which now occupies the yard, surrounded by a red brick deck and patio.

Because the side yards were too narrow and access was restricted, excavation equipment could not be brought to the site and the five-foot-deep pool had to be dug entirely by hand. The excavated earth was used to form a level area for entertainment to one side of the pool. The red brick paving extends into the entertainment area, which is reached through an opening in the eugenia hedge that runs the length of the pool. Two miniature Egyptian obelisks flank this opening to indicate its significance as an entry.

The pool itself is an example of how the use of materials, architectural accessories, and plantings can formalize a space, creating an outdoor room. Broad precast coping outlines the dark rectangle of the pool against the brick deck. The coping leads the eye the length of the pool to the focal point—a flight of five broad steps up to a raised patio shaded by Hawaiian treeferns. On either side of the steps stand two cast goats acquired at an auction at the Metro-Goldwyn-Mayer movie studios after the statues had appeared in such films as *Marie Antoinette* (1938) with Norma Shearer and *Singing in the Rain* (1952) with Gene Kelly. Now they trickle water into the Wilkinson pool as part of the recirculating and filtering system.

The stark outlining and symmetry of the pool's basic structure is softened by the oriental jars and urns that line the edges and introduce fine detail and eye-catching color, yet maintain the balance of the overall scheme. White geraniums add visual interest and scent without interrupting the serenity of the area with bright colors.

The pool's landscaping offers multiple options for entertaining. At the top of the flight of steps waits a table and chairs for romantic, candle-lit dining at poolside. On festive occasions a crystal chandelier is hung from a large tree, making the setting seem part of the enchanted Arabian Nights.

Above: Two cast-metal goats, retired from the movie business, flank the steps to a shaded dining area.

Left: The painted detail of the oriental jars seems to mingle with the fine reflection of the trees.

THE LANGUAGE OF ORNAMENT: THE ZODIAC POOL

The entire bottom of the pool is a huge mosaic, a glorious burst of intricate
design representing the twelve signs of the zodiac.

The curve of the overlapping steps accentuates the design of the mosaic, which stretches out into the fan-shaped pool.

During and following the Great Depression there were still some people other than movie stars, directors, and producers who had the means to build opulent homes and pools in the Beverly Hills, Bel Air, and Holmby Hills area. One such individual was Jay Paley, president of the Columbia Broadcasting System. In 1936 Paley created one of the most impressive estates in Southern California on a wedge-shaped site just west of Angelo Drive in Holmby Hills.

The residence was designed by architect Paul Williams in a restrained yet exquisitely detailed American Colonial style, and the gardens and the extraordinary swimming pool were designed by Edward Huntsman-Trout, who was one of Southern California's most successful landscape architects.

Huntsman-Trout planned a series of formal gardens around the Paley mansion, and at the end of a broad expanse of lawn he placed the swimming pool—a pool that became the estate's pièce de résistance, overshadowing both the grand residence and the lavish gardens.

Previous pages: Sunlight shining through
the water makes the mosaic seem to shimmer;
the wave-like steps add to this illusion of
movement.

The glass doors of the pool house open
onto a small patio, with a view across the pool
and lawn toward the main house.

The entire bottom of the pool is a
huge mosaic, a glorious burst of intricate
design. At the bottom of the curved,
intertwined access steps the tiles form a
golden sunburst which extends out into
the blue mosaic to form yet another,
more elaborate sunburst, interspersed
with illuminated circles, each representing one of the twelve signs of the
zodiac. On one side of the pool is a pool
house whose tall glass doors open onto
the narrow deck.

In the 1960s the Paley estate lost about
half of its original acreage to subdivision,
but due to the lay of the land and the
screen provided by trees planted by
Huntsman-Trout, the remarkable swimming pool and pool house retain their
original splendor and privacy.

CHAPTER SIX

POOLS WITH A VIEW

The view from a pool is as important as the appearance of the pool itself.
Of primary importance is, of course, the choice of location…

…but equally important is the land-scaping. The right trees must be chosen and placed in such a way that they do not obstruct the view.

In fact, careful landscaping can channel the eye toward the best possible vista, framing it and thereby increasing its beauty.

California pools offer a broad menu of wooded, mountain, ocean, countryside, or urban views. From the hills of Tiburon near San Francisco there is a stunning view of the Golden Gate Bridge, and

many a pool in the Santa Monica Mountains looks out over Hollywood or the San Fernando Valley—at night a carpet of glittering multi-hued jewels lies spread out before the swimmer.

POOLS WITH A VIEW: LOBO CANYON

The pool and pool house designed by the landscape architectural firm Campbell & Campbell
for Leah and Paul Culberg are situated on a ridge in the Santa Monica Mountains
with a commanding view of one distinctive peak, and Lobo Canyon below.

Water from the spa in the foreground trickles down a rocky waterfall and into the pool. Stones with gray-green coppery veins, used in the pool house and around the pool, were collected from the creek in the valley.

The pool and pool house designed by the landscape architectural firm Campbell & Campbell for Leah and Paul Culberg are situated on a ridge in the Santa Monica Mountains with a commanding view of one distinctive peak, and Lobo Canyon below. The pool house was placed so it would block a neighboring house from view, allowing an uninterrupted natural vista from the pool.

The Culbergs acquired their ten-acre parcel of an original ranch, the Boyd Ranch, in 1976. The old ranch house, built in 1920 without any modern amenities, was still standing, and the Culbergs moved in. When the devastating Malibu fire of 1978 gutted the ranch house beyond repair, it took the Culbergs until 1980 to rebuild. In 1993 they added the pool and the pool house, built of the same local stones as the original ranch house.

When the pool was ready to be filled, the Culbergs discovered that there was insufficient well water available, and they had to use water from the creek a hundred feet below the pool. This was accomplished with a water ladder consisting of three large garbage cans placed on different levels of the steep slope, a hundred feet of hose, and four pumps relaying the water from the creek to the lowest can, from can to can, and finally to the pool.

The opening in the wall at the end of the pool facing the peak leads to a flight of stairs which descends to a rose garden and a *glorietta*, a Mexican gazebo, on the slope below.

At the opposite end, a spa, raised five steps above the pool, is connected with it by a flow-through waterfall set with geodes found near the site. Local masons familiar with the geodes imbedded them so the crystals catch the morning sun.

The propane-heated pool has a cover, which can be rolled up and stored out of sight in an aluminum housing under the deck on the mountain-end of the pool. The cover can be operated from the pool house, which offers a clear view of the pool to prevent any possible accidents. Since fire is always a danger in the mountains, the pool house also holds a fire pump, which in an emergency can be rolled out to the pool, where a hose can dip into the water.

The Culberg pool is in daily use—invigorating in the morning and restful in the evening, when the purple afterglow of the sunset tints the mountains pastel colors and in the early summer the cries of mountain lions echo through the canyons.

POOLS WITH A VIEW: LAKE SHERWOOD

High on the slope above Lake Sherwood in Ventura County north of Los Angeles,
a natural pool dominated by an eight-foot waterfall offers a panoramic view
that makes the entire lake below seem part of the rocky pool.

All the rocks around the pool are artificial, and contain pockets for plants.

High on the slope above Lake Sherwood in Ventura County north of Los Angeles, a natural pool dominated by an eight-foot waterfall offers a panoramic view that makes the entire lake below seem part of the rocky pool.

Although neighboring properties are located on the hillside below, the pool is designed so they cannot be seen, making the pool site limitless.

The owner of the pool had a very small backyard, but requested a pool as large as possible without overwhelming the property. Architect Mark L. Smith and pool builder Bill Brooks, owner of Rock Designs, Inc., designed an irregularly shaped, rock-enclosed pool directly on the property line facing the lake. It is twenty-five feet at its longest and twelve feet at its widest, and incorporates a waterfall and a large grotto, which contains an eight-by-eight-foot spa. The water for the waterfall is recirculated from the pool and is fed from a small pond located on top of the grotto.

The pool area is illuminated by low-voltage lights above and inside the grotto, and underwater lighting comes from quartz halogen lights, two in the pool and one in the spa. Quartz halogen was used because the light is white rather than yellow.

From the small rock-paved patio between the pool and the house, the soothing sound of the waterfall combines with the view of the pool, lake, and wooded mountains beyond to suggest a private wilderness.

POOLS WITH A VIEW: THE PALO ALTO HILLS

The view from this hilltop pool just south of San Francisco is secure for many years to come
because the pastoral countryside is owned by the Palo Alto municipality,
which has declared it shall never be developed.

The view from this hilltop pool just
south of San Francisco is secure for
many years to come because the pastoral
countryside is owned by the Palo Alto
municipality, which has declared it shall
never be developed.

The native oak trees that adorn the hills
are protected by law, which declares that
every oak with a circumference of four
feet or more is a Heritage Tree.

Designed by landscape architect
Peter Wright Shaw and built by Tim
McDonough of Silvercreek Development,
the pool is forty-three by twenty-three
feet with a depth ranging from three and
one-half feet to nine feet. An offset section
eleven by eight feet is only eighteen
inches deep. From there the water spills
over a weir in a ten-foot waterfall.
Originally only a short, quiet fall over the
infinity edge was planned, but during
construction the fall was made longer so
it would cascade noisily over a wall of
craggy rocks. A path was built to view the
fall from below.

In the offset section of the pool is a
circular spa eight feet in diameter. Its
raised rim is made of blue tiles except for
the part of the circumference that faces
the house. That portion is set with glass
blocks which shine at night when the spa
is lit. The spa can be reached from the
pool deck by two pedestal stepping stones
just below the surface of the water, one
on each side of the spa. Sunk into the

Submerged stepping stones lead to the spa,
which is heated to 104 degrees every night by
a computerized system.

bottom of the spa is a fountain that can rise in three telescopic sections to the water's surface and spout a fleur-de-lis-patterned spray into the air, confined to the circle of the spa. At night the illuminated pool and the spa with the lighted fountain are spectacular.

The pool is plastered dove gray, with a rim of handmade tiles in a custom dark gray, which seems to disappear in the shadow under the lip of the pool. Dove gray was chosen for the pool instead of black because black-plastered pools tend to mottle, although mottling is sometimes seen as an advantage in natural pools.

Although the pool and spa are on the same control system for ease of maintenance, a computerized system of valves heats the spa alone to a temperature of 104 degrees every night at six o'clock so bathers can relax at the end of the day and enjoy the serene countryside surrounding the property.

In some affluent residences in California the indoor swimming pool has become increasingly popular. The indoor pool allows the pool owner options of opulent design and ornamentation not possible outdoors, as well as the conveniences of shelter, privacy, and security, and the possibility of comfortable year-round use.

European and American indoor pools built around 1900 were heavily influenced by a desire to emulate the classic Roman baths and pools and the later elegant European spas with their exaggerated appurtenances—from Pompeian columns and narrow balconies to rubber mats and crystal chandeliers—and regardless of their shortcomings in efficiency and convenience. By the 1950s, however, the tremendously heightened interest in both public and private outdoor pools piqued interest in efficient and economical indoor pools as well.

The indoor pool offers control. The temperature of both the pool and its enclosure can be adjusted; there are no weather considerations at any time of year; interior light sources (which must meet basic local codes and regulations)

make it possible to swim at night— brightly illuminated, or with romantically subdued lighting; and maintenance is reduced to a minimum, since leaves and other flying debris are not present.

Ideally, indoor pools should be built simultaneously with the residence, when incorporating ideas into the design is easiest. When an indoor pool is added to a preexisting home, this pool can be constructed as an attached enclosure that complements the appearance of the house, or an independent structure that houses the pool. Construction is similar to that of any other type of pool.

Although indoor pools offer many advantages, they also present some disadvantages, foremost of which is, of course, the loss of the outdoor setting. Special problems also arise in the circulation and ventilation of air in the pool area. The

CHAPTER SEVEN

INDOOR WATERS

moisture and heat in the interior space produces a greenhouse effect, which can make the air virtually unbreatheable. Air conditioning and proper ventilation can alleviate this problem. Ventilation can be provided by a natural system or a mechanical system, which should be separate from that of the main house. Natural ventilation may require adjustable vents, and shades in the summer, while mechanical ventilation requires equipment such as wall-mounted fans. The systems for drainage, water supply, and filtration are the same as for other pools. Finally, care must be taken that pool water does not come in contact with rugs or floors, which will be bleached or stained by the chemicals in the water. A poolside shower or an area for thoroughly drying off can help avoid this problem.

Many of these same principles apply to the less common indoor/outdoor pool—a pool that spans both spaces. There are two ways of designing such a pool. One option is to create an indoor setting that is solely for use with the pool. This space can be connected directly to the main residence and can be comfortably and imaginatively furnished with amenities such as television, bar, vented barbeque, even a spa, but it is a separate living space, and any problems inherent to the indoor pool do not enter into the dwelling area proper.

The second option is to build part of the pool into the living space itself, making it a feature of the interior design. To shield the interior from outside elements such as cold, rain, or fog, a partition, usually glass, separates the inside from the outside. This partition can be movable, sliding across the water to open up the pool, or it can be stationary, dipping into the water to provide a seal, requiring the swimmer to dive under it to pass from one side to the other.

Security is assured by a system of alarm beams which detects the motion of any intruder. One variation on this established security system is an alarm system that detects any object or body that enters or falls into the pool. This is primarily meant for the safety of children, but it also makes an excellent alarm against unwanted intruders. Some indoor/outdoor pools have no partition to shelter the interior space, which is more in the nature of a porte cochere, and is not included in the security system for the rest of the house.

In many ways indoor pools diminish for their owners one of California's unique offerings—the possibility of outdoor living—but they do offer those with the means to build them a way of ignoring nature's demands. They can be particularly convenient in areas with cold winters, strong winds, or regular rains. Whatever the motivation for an indoor pool, it is a rare luxury to be able to take a sheltered swim at any moment, day or night.

The recently renovated aquamarine pool is surrounded by an ornate tiled wainscot
with the geometric intricacy of an oriental carpet.

The pool enclosure has the appearance of a courtyard, as indeed it can be when the roof is open, exposing the pool room to the sky.

A few miles south of Santa Barbara at the base of the Santa Ynez Mountains, facing the Santa Barbara Channel, is one of the most spectacular indoor swimming pools in California—the splendid, twenty-by-sixty-foot Moorish-style natatorium built in 1927 for the multimillionaire playboy Albert K. Isham. This pool is so distinctive that it has been designated Santa Barbara County Landmark No. 28.

Designed by George Washington Smith, who was considered the most talented of the 1920s Spanish Colonial revivalist architects active in the Santa Barbara and Pasadena area, the recently renovated aquamarine pool is surrounded by an ornate tiled wainscot with the geometric intricacy of an oriental carpet. The tile mural on the north wall behind a small fountain that stands in the pool itself depicts brilliantly colored fish and seahorses among the coral of an imaginative seaworld. The magnificent tile scenes bordering a fireplace at the opposite end of the pool are taken from the motifs of Persian miniatures. To this day the origin of these tiles remains a mystery. The opinion of architect Henry Lenny, who worked on the recent restoration of the pool, supports the notation on Smith's original plans that specifies "Tunisian tiles." Indeed, Smith specified or designed everything in the pool area, even the colored lucite towel bars in the bath and shower rooms, which represent a very early use of lucite. The deck that surrounds the pool is paved with hexagonal, bronze-colored tiles. The roof is retractable to

The elaborate tiles might be Tunisian,
but their true origin remains a mystery.

expose swimmers to the sun or to the moon and stars, and rich oriental lighting fixtures inspired by Moorish lanterns illuminate the pool at night.

Outlined on the bottom of the pool in blue tiles are five four-foot-wide swimming lanes. The filling and overflow systems are regulated by scum gutters ringing the pool. For the recent restoration by preservationist David Sheldon, the pool's stature as a landmark saved it from having to be brought up to code, which might have required new electric wiring, plumbing, or methods of access.

In 1947 the main house, which was Normandy-style to conform with the surrounding houses at the time, was washed out to sea in a storm, but the pool structure survived. It was built of poured concrete before gunite was available, and is now further protected by a seawall. Today the pool is part of the communal area of a showcase housing development. It is not open to the public, but is occasionally rented out as a motion picture location or for special events in the spirit of its legendary history: anecdote has it that Isham once drove his Duesenberg into the pool, with a beautiful starlet sipping champagne perched on each front fender.

Tiled scenes from Persian miniatures surround a fireplace in the vaulted and horseshoe-arched entrance.

The owners of a residence in Seacliff, San Francisco wanted to remodel the large garage partially dug into the hillside beneath their home and convert it into an indoor swimming pool, but they had one minor request.

The owners of a residence in Seacliff, San Francisco wanted to remodel the large garage partially dug into the hillside beneath their home and convert it into an indoor swimming pool, but they had one minor request: they wanted the new pool to have the feel of the famous indoor Roman Pool at Hearst Castle in San Simeon. This was no easy task, especially since there was not a single right angle in the asymmetrical garage space—making the symmetric formality of rhythmic arches and Palladian proportions difficult to achieve. The first challenge would be to create the illusion of symmetry, which is the foundation of classicism in design. This challenge fell upon designers Sid DelMar Leach and his wife April of Leach & Leach.

It was all done with mirrors. First, by request of the owners, the pool was made as large as possible with a minimal deck around it. One sharply angled corner of the space was truncated and a false, mirrored door was placed in the resulting short wall to balance the single entry to the pool area at the other end of the room. The existing structural pilasters were transformed into giant tile-embellished torcheres, and five operable steel and glass double doors were installed to lead to the outside garden and courtyard.

To achieve the desired grandeur and aid in providing a classic, repeating rhythm to the space, *faux marbre* columns flank the doors around the pool perimeter. These columns and the upper wall panels are painted to match the real Norwegian Rose marble at the column bases and on the floor. The ceiling is a shallow formed-in-place plaster dome which rises eleven and one-half feet above the pool surface. The soffit which visibly supports the dome houses air diffuser components, which pull the moist air out of the pool area. The color of the ceiling is graduated from light blue at the perimeter to sky blue in the center, recreating the appearance of the natural sky.

The colors used in the pool area were also influenced by nature's palette. Tiles were acquired from five countries, and include fourteen-carat gold border tiles from Japan, eighteen-carat gold waterproof tiles from France, twelve-by-twelve-inch marble tiles, and matched sets of hand-painted arabesque tiles. The twelve-by-six-foot oval medallion set in tiles in the bottom of the blue-plastered pool was designed by Del Leach, and is made with Brazilian glass mosaic tiles in four colors.

Completed in 1990, the pool is twenty-nine feet long at its longest and twenty-four feet wide at its widest, with a uniform depth of four feet. Rather than containing chlorine, the water is purified by a new system of forced ozone purification.

The only artificial lighting in the pool area comes from the torcheres, four alabaster sconces mounted on the blue-tiled wall panels and the underwater lighting, which combine to create a moody, romantic ambience. A speaker system brings music into the pool area so the owners can swim to Beethoven, Brahms, and Wagner. The dome overhead directs the sound so that it can be heard underwater.

Working and non-operable arched double doors, some of them mirrored, contribute to the symmetry of this pool, which is modeled after the Roman Pool at Hearst Castle.

INDOOR WATERS: WOODSIDE

Housed in a light-filled, columned structure, the raised pool is inspired by
a European health spa pool.

Twenty-seven underground piers of reinforced concrete support the pool addition on the unstable hillside.

The owners of a residence and outdoor swimming pool in San Mateo County near San Francisco decided they wanted to swim in comfort year-round, and built an indoor swimming pool attached to their house.

The house is situated on a gently sloping hillside, and the excavation for the pool and a small outdoor patio was dug on the slope below the house, so that the roof of the pool structure became a terrace at ground level in front of the residence. A flight of steps connects the little patio below, adjoining the pool, to the terrace and garden above. Because the hillside soil is unstable, twenty-seven massive piers of reinforced concrete sixteen inches in diameter were set ten feet deep into the ground to support the structure being built.

Housed in a light-filled, columned structure, the raised pool is thirty-nine by nine feet, with a depth of four and one-half feet. The owners had seen and photographed a European health spa pool, which became the inspiration for their own. Timothy McDonough of Silvercreek Development, the construction firm on the project, surfaced the pool in dark green color-customized standard tiles whose color lightens as they march down the inside pool wall, until they are almost white on the bottom. McDonough used four-by-one-half-inch tiles to achieve the smooth progression over the broad, soft-rolled edge of the pool, so that it looks like the scaled back of a giant lizard.

The water washes over the rounded edge of the pool and flows down the outside pool walls. The overflow water is collected in a six-inch-wide gutter that rings the pool. From here the water is channeled to a thousand-gallon holding tank for recirculation, or for storage when the weir is not in operation. Because this weir constantly brings the water right to the top edge of the pool walls, the pool appears to be a self-contained block of dark water.

The pool is equipped with a current machine so swimmers can swim in place. At one end of the pool is an eight-by-six-foot spa with the same contours and materials as the pool itself. Adjoining the area are a steam room, a sauna, and an exercise room—a modified version of the European spa admired by the owners.

Because of the rounded weir edge,
to the swimmer the pool looks like a wall-less
block of water.

INDOOR WATERS: CORONA DEL MAR

The highly unusual house is built around a long, meandering swimming pool
which is partly outdoors and partly inside a protected space where the house
overhangs it and surrounds it on three sides.

A Japanese-style circular gate leads from the pool to a walkway around the house.

When Etsuko and Joe Price saw the work of Bart Prince, an Albuquerque, New Mexico architect whose distinctive style had achieved international renown, they immediately knew that he was the man to design their new home and pool, to be constructed on a small landspit in Corona del Mar, overlooking the ocean.

The highly unusual house is built around a long, meandering swimming pool which is partly outdoors and partly inside a protected space where the house overhangs it and surrounds it on three sides. The pool is shaped like a long, twice-knotted balloon, forming three connecting pool segments. At the narrow points, two curved bridges span the water. Half of the pool system is outdoors, and offers access to the living/dining room, the master bedroom, a playroom, and the kitchen, as well as the garage. The second story of the house swirls around and over the pool courtyard in an undulating form of wood shingles, glue-laminated wood strips, and wood-and-copper siding in the natural hues of the materials, and overhangs the other half of the pool system.

The upper floor, reached by a wooden spiral stairway that rises out of the inner pool segment, holds an entertainment room, a bar, and an office. This inner pool segment has a spa, and at the outer segment a waterfall cascades into the pool over boulders and rocks.

All three pool segments are tiled white. They have raised, amply rounded rims, tiled with small Japanese tiles, and the decking around them is dark, polished granite, which is harder and more resistant than marble and tolerates chlorine better. The granite is lightly sandblasted for safety, but still retains some of its lustre. Around the inside rims the two innermost pool segments have broad edges for wading, twelve inches below the water's surface. They are tiled with the same dark granite as the deck. At sixteen feet across, the center pool segment is the widest, and the bottlenecks spanned by the bridges are eight feet across. The depths of the pool segments range from three feet to nine feet at the waterfall in the outer pool segment. Here, a Japanese-style circular gate leads outside the courtyard to a walkway around the house.

The house and the forty-five-foot-long string of connected pools are solar heated, the hot water flowing in pipes through the heat exchange tank, and the pool water recirculating from the waterfall. An electric heating system is also available if needed.

The Prices had requested that the pool be an integral part of the residence, both spectacularly decorative and well suited for swimming. It took from 1984 to 1987 to complete the project, but the result is a success—a lively space where, as Bart Prince intended, it is difficult to discern inside from outside.

The unusual design marries biomorphic and mechanical elements.

The carefully placed elements in the
courtyard suggest the language of
the Japanese rock garden.

INDOOR WATERS: SOUTH RIDGE

A few feet in from the pool's rim, two curved sliding glass partitions
skim over the water's surface to enclose the indoor section of the pool.

The pool joins a terrace indoors.
An outdoor terrace can be seen beyond
the curved partitions.

On a ridge with a breathtaking view of
Palm Springs stands a house and an
indoor/outdoor pool designed in 1971 by
famed California architect John Lautner
for interior designer Arthur Elrod. Palm
Springs is surrounded by the Agua
Caliente Indian Reservation, and here
on the site of the Elrod house and pool,
Native Americans may have stood a
hundred years before the house was
built, watching the stage coach stop
below on the route between Prescott,
Arizona and Los Angeles.

In 1996 after the house had been standing
unoccupied for several years, a new owner
conscientiously restored the property with
the help of North East Builders, a firm
that specializes in historic restoration.

The pool is an integral part of the
poured-in-place concrete residential
structure. Viewed from below, the half-
moon-shaped pool structure resembles a
one-story-high concrete barrel. The water
from the pool spills over the semi-circular
rim and flows down the massive concrete containing wall to be gathered in a
holding pond below for recirculation.
There, a system added during the
restoration purifies the water before
returning it to the pool. This spectacular
weir was an early use of the infinity
pool principle by the visionary Lautner.
Against the cylindrical wall of the pool
structure is a metal sculpture and a series
of jet sprays that can be activated to
hit the sculpture's blades and play them
like a wind chime.

The barrel-shaped structure that contains
the pool is an integral part of the form of the
house, which is designed on a loose series
of three circles. One contains the parking court,
sculpture garden, and entryway at the front
of the house; the second, central circle contains
the living and dining rooms; and the third
is the smaller partial circle of the pool
at the back of the house.

The interior of the pool is plastered black, both for improved heat conservation and to reflect the beautiful sky; the pool is gas heated and the deck around it has been restored to its natural salt-finished concrete. Half the pool extends into the house and is met by a terrace just a few steps down from the living room. A few feet in from the pool's rim, two large, curved sliding glass partitions form a barrier, skimming over the water's surface to enclose the indoor section of the pool. The swimmer can duck under the closed partition to enjoy an indoor or an outdoor swim, or the partition can be opened from the computerized pool-equipment controls in the house.

This innovative pool that ties inside to out carries on the theme of the house, which is established by rocky outcroppings from the hillside into the rooms, and the immense concrete spokes of the roof, which frame wedge-shaped windows offering views of the distant mountains.

When the curved partitions are open, the panoramic view from the terrace is spectacular.

153

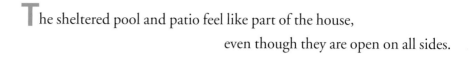

The sheltered pool and patio feel like part of the house,
even though they are open on all sides.

Mexican architect Ricardo Legorreta designed this vacation house in San Diego County, the indoor/outdoor swimming pool, and the surrounding landscaping. Built in 1987, the pool is as much part of the architecture of the project as is the house itself. This pool is really two connected pools, one a thirty-five-by-thirty rectangular pool, and the other a lap pool forty-five feet long and seven and one-half feet wide.

Part of the large pool is sheltered by a louvered overhang extending from a solid ceiling over the patio area that connects to the house. A seven-by-seven-foot spa and the access steps to the pool are next to the covered patio area, and the lap pool extends beyond the louvered overhang to a fountain and small waterfall at the far end, creating a swimming lane eighty feet long. The swimming lane has an olympic gutter detail that allows the water to fall away from the swimmer so there is no surge resistance in the narrow pool.

The wall that divides the sheltered pool from the open-air portion effectively creates a sense of enclosure for the patio and the spa, designating these areas as part of the house, even though they have no walls. At the same time, the wings of the pool that push beyond this "enclosure" provide a link to the open spaces beyond.

The design of the pool area reflects a variation on the original design by Legorreta and his clients due to a need to strike a compromise with nature. The expansive lawn area which extends right up to the edge of the pool deck was first planted with an attractive, low ground cover. This ground cover provided concealment for snakes, however, which slithered out to sun themselves on the warm, French limestone decking, risking undesirable encounters with swimmers. The snakes' presence therefore dictated a design alteration from ground cover to the present short grass—a good solution for all involved!

Two solid walls and the covered patio area on one side of the large pool make it feel like an indoor space.

The outdoor space—pools, terraces,
lawn—is divided into rooms, just as inside
the house.

The wings of the pool that push
beyond the sheltered sections lead the eye to
the open landscape in the distance.

Among the many thousands of residential swimming pools built in California since the early years of the twentieth century, a select few have gained historical prominence—based on the prominence of their owners, or based on innovations of design made by vanguard architects and landscape designers.

For sheer scale and grandeur, the foremost of these famous pools has to be the Neptune Pool at William Randolph Hearst's San Simeon estate in San Luis Obispo County. The Donnell pool in Sonoma is known for its innovative free-form design, which was instrumental in breaking the conventional swimming pool out of its rectangular mold.

Newsworthy owners or unusual designs are also tickets to fame for pools such as the grand piano-shaped pool with keyboard-tile decking built in Encino by Liberace, or the heart-shaped pool with its message—"I love you, Jayne"—set in large tiles on the bottom, which belonged to the motion picture actress Jayne Mansfield.

Whatever feature catches the public eye—architectural importance, glittering wealth, good taste or bad—California pools have set a social and architectural precedent for the rest of the world to admire.

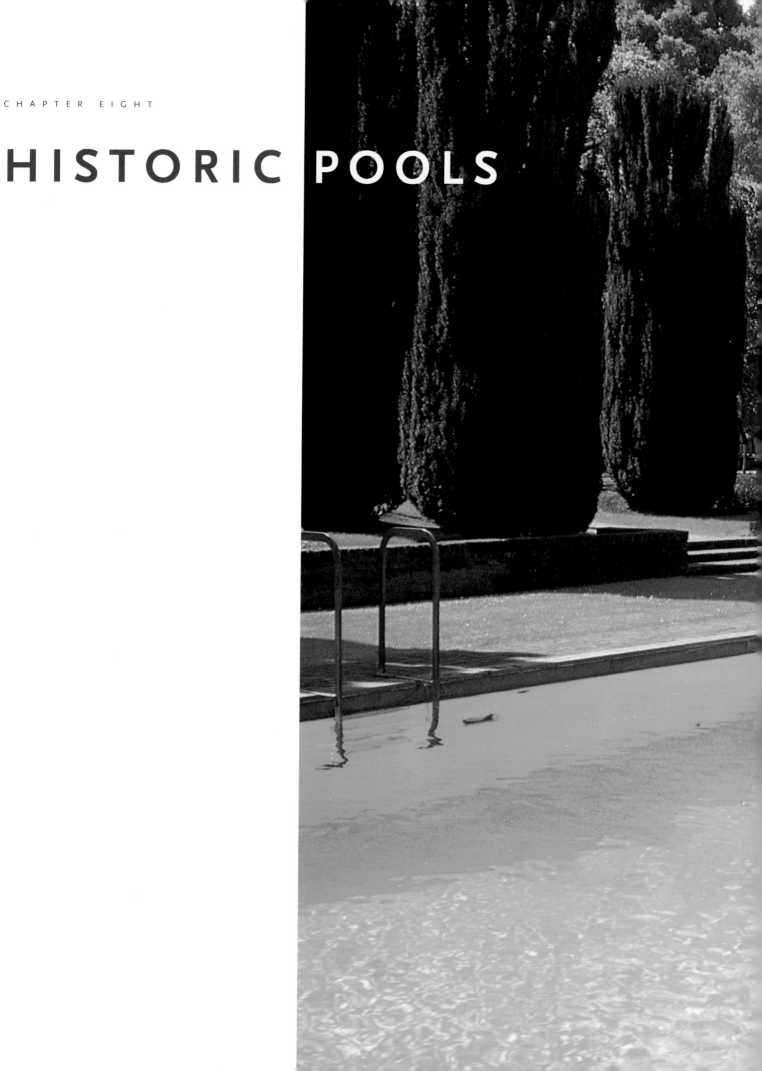

CHAPTER EIGHT

HISTORIC POOLS

The estate of department store tycoon Harry Winchester Robinson and his wife Virginia featured the first swimming pool in an area which decades later would boast thousands.

Built in 1927, this fifty-by-twenty-foot rectangular swimming pool is part of the celebrated Virginia Robinson Gardens located on a hill outside Los Angeles in what is now Beverly Hills. The estate of department store tycoon Harry Winchester Robinson and his wife Virginia featured the first swimming pool in an area which decades later would boast thousands.

The Robinsons returned from their honeymoon in 1906, enamored of the gardens of Italy and Spain, and Virginia's father, architect Nathaniel Dryden, built the couple a Mediterranean classic revival house in 1911 as a wedding gift. From there developed the estate which opened to the public in 1982 as the Virginia Robinson Gardens, and constitutes an important contribution to Southern California garden history. The gardens themselves were suggested to the Robinsons in 1921 by landscape architect Charles Gibbs Adams, who became their principal designer. The gardens cover six sloping acres and feature a two-and-one-half-acre semi-tropical palm grove.

The pool is located in the northwest area of the gardens, and is completely lined with white three-quarter-inch tiles, giving way to a border of rust-colored tiles at the gutter. A row of inset tiles announces the depth of the pool: four feet, five, eight, nine, then eight again at the elegantly ornamented wall with fountain which fronts the pool pavilion and forms the north side of the pool.

The elaborate pavilion is a miniature version of a Palladian villa for the Pisani family, near Venice, Italy. It has dark-stained ceiling beams stenciled in black, marble floors in a checkerboard pattern, and a huge fireplace and hearth.

The deck around the pool is in terra-cotta tiles of various sizes, and the eight-inch border on the three sides of the pool is raised four inches above the deck. The pool is not heated, and never was, but is equipped with a modern filtration system. The original system consisted of huge cast-iron drums containing progressively finer grades of sand through which the water was pumped for filtration. This same type of system is still used in the Neptune Pool and the Roman Pool belonging to William Randolph Hearst (page 163). The original drums are still in place at the Robinson Pool.

In the sixty-six years of Virginia Robinson's residence, the house and grounds grew to represent an era of gracious living and the Robinsons' legendary hospitality. Today the pool is seldom used for swimming, but is a showplace on the Virginia Robinson Gardens tours, and the site of many festivities.

The elaborate pavilion is a miniature version of Villa Pisani, near Venice.

One of the most widely photographed and written-about swimming pools, not only in California, but in the entire world, is the pool of truly heroic proportions at San Simeon, or Hearst Castle, which crowns a spur of the Santa Lucia Mountains overlooking the Pacific Ocean.

One of the most widely photographed and written-about swimming pools, not only in California, but in the entire world, is the pool of truly heroic proportions at San Simeon, or Hearst Castle, which crowns a spur of the Santa Lucia Mountains overlooking the Pacific Ocean.

Today the castle and its grounds are a state historical monument.

Designed and built for the fabled newspaper tycoon William Randolph Hearst (1863–1951) by the San Francisco-based architect Julia Morgan (1872–1957) the pool was under construction from 1934 to 1936. Morgan was the state's first licensed woman architect, and had already achieved fame with her first individual commission, a bell tower on the campus of Mills College in Oakland (1904), one of the very few major structures that withstood the devastating earthquake of 1906. The Hearst Castle and the Neptune Pool were to become the most memorable of all her designs.

Three successive pools were built on the site. In 1924 the original clover-leaf-shaped garden pool was nearly complete when Hearst instructed Julia Morgan to redesign and enlarge it into a swimming pool, which was done in 1926–27. It was a large oval pool with a cascade running down a series of concrete steps at one end. Eight years later the present Neptune Pool, an expansion of the oval pool, was begun when Hearst wanted his pool to be a little more imposing.

A grand staircase leads down to the magnificent pool from the level above, where the house is located. The pool is 104 feet long and 58 feet wide with an alcove which makes the width at that point 95 feet. Though the pool is only three and one-half feet deep, it holds 350,000 gallons of water.

Opposite the alcove, which contains a waterfall and a marble statue of Venus, stands a Greco-Roman temple facade in granite and marble with Corinthian columns and a carved entablature, against a backdrop of wooded hills. In the center of the pediment stands the figure of Neptune, Roman god of the seas, who lends his name to this grandiose pool. Etruscan-style colonnades at each end of the pool and white marble statuary that rests on pedestals at the pool's edges complete the classic setting, and reflect Morgan's Beaux-Arts training.

The entire pool area is constructed with marble—the pool and colonnades are light-veined Vermont marble and verde antique serpentinite, also from Vermont. In Hearst's time the pool was heated year-round by big oil burners. Today it is not heated, since it is no longer used for swimming, but the original filtering system is still in use.

The other famous swimming pool at San Simeon is the Roman Pool, the huge indoor pool built beneath the tennis court for use in foggy or inclement weather. Also designed by Julia Morgan, it is lighted by alabaster globes, richly tiled in lapis lazuli and gold leaf, and watched over by white marble nudes. Construction cost over a million dollars and was completed in 1934, the year construction began on the Neptune Pool. Still, the Neptune Pool was the favorite of Hearst's guests—which included such illustrious personalities as Amelia Earhart, Charles Lindbergh, Greta Garbo, and Bing Crosby—and the Roman Pool was left for use by the service personnel who maintained the huge estate.

The namesake of the Neptune Pool stands in the center of the pediment of the granite and marble Greco-Roman temple.

HISTORIC POOLS: THE BEVERLY HOUSE POOL

With its recent renovation and its appearance in several motion pictures,
the Beverly House pool is once again one of the most legendary pools in California.

Marion Davies brought statuary from Hearst's San Simeon for the lawns around her own Venetian-inspired pool.

In the business and entertainment heyday of the 1920s Beverly Hills was home to numerous legendary motion picture superstars such as Douglas Fairbanks Sr. and Mary Pickford, Harold Lloyd, and Charlie Chaplin, and successful businessmen such as automobile magnate Errett Lobban Cord, oil millionaire Edward Laurence Doheny Jr., who constructed the Greystone mansion in Truesdale, and banker Milton Getz—owner of the residence later known as the Beverly House.

In 1925 Getz purchased an orchard at the foot of Coldwater Canyon and hired architect Gordon Kaufmann to design what was to become the *dernier cri* of 1920s architectural opulence. He engaged landscape architect Paul Thiene to design the elegant and extensive gardens surrounding the mansion and the striking pool behind it.

Beginning at a large terrace behind the mansion, Thiene placed two long, narrow reflecting pools that step down the gentle incline in a series of placid waterfalls which flow into the large swimming pool. The pool can hold 100,000 gallons of water, and is thirty by seventy feet and plunges to a depth of fourteen feet, with a series of underwater steps that run the full width of the pool where the water from the reflecting pools splashes into it. An apron of cast concrete surrounds the pool, which Thiene placed in a dramatic setting with three Moorish-style pavilions and great expanses of luxurious green lawn. He lined the entire area with stately palms and evergreens, and beyond it designed three different, adjacent gardens.

But the Depression was not kind to Milton Getz, and he was forced to sell his home. At the end of World War II the lavish mansion stood unoccupied, the grand pool empty, when a guardian angel appeared on the scene. Her name was Marion Davies—the blonde former movie star, by then an intimate companion of newspaper mogul William Randolph Hearst. In 1947 she bought the estate for the munificent sum of $200,000. She thoroughly renovated the estate and brought statuary from San Simeon for the lawns at the pool. Shortly thereafter she moved in with WR, as she called Hearst, who left his beloved San Simeon to be nearer to the Beverly Hills physicians.

Their stay together in the Beverly House, as Hearst called it, was not long. When Hearst died in 1951, Davies stayed on and eventually remarried. Upon her death in 1961, her widower, Captain Horace Brown, began to rent out the mansion and the magnificent pool as film and television locations. In 1966 the lower portion of the estate grounds were sold off and subdivided, and ultimately the Beverly House was sold as well.

In recent years, the swimming pool, which is newly retiled, and the restored mansion and grounds have been seen in several motion pictures such as *The Godfather* (1972) with Marlon Brando, and *The Body Guard* (1993) with Kevin Costner and Whitney Houston—reestablishing the Beverly House pool as one of the most recognized and legendary pools in California.

The rectangular pool looks like a sky-blue gem in its setting

of a red-brick border and green, flawlessly manicured lawn.

The pool at Filoli is significant not in itself, although it possesses a dignity and simple elegance of its own, but because of its close connection with a historically important estate. Located thirty miles south of San Francisco on the eastern slope of the Coast Range, Filoli is one of the last remaining, beautifully preserved and internationally famous grand country estates of the early twentieth century.

Both the modified Georgian-style mansion and the world-renowned series of gardens laid out in an Italian/French-based system of parterres, terraces, lawns, and reflecting pools, were built in 1916–19 by a prominent San Francisco couple, Mr. and Mrs. William B. Bourn II, whose wealth came from the Empire Gold Mine in Grass Valley. William Bourn had a credo: "Fight for a just cause, love your fellow man and live a good life." He named his estate by taking the first two letters from each of the governing words: FIght, LOve, LIve—FILOLI. Private swimming pools were not yet common, and the Filoli pool was added at a later date.

Architect Willis Polk designed the residence, and Bruce Porter, known for his garden designs, planned the Filoli gardens, with Isabella Worms supervising the planting. Working closely with the Bourns, Porter created a concourse of formal gardens with a wealth of trees, shrubbery, and hedges; wisterias, Chilean myrtle, rhododendrons, and camelias (new to California gardens at the time), lilies, magnolias, roses, and dozens of exotic blooms.

In 1975 the estate was donated to the National Trust for Historic Preservation.

After the Bourns passed away, the estate was bought by Lurline and William P. Roth in 1937. Mrs. Roth, an avid and knowledgeable horticulturist, took over the love and care of the Filoli gardens, for which she was awarded the Distinguished Service Medal of the Garden Club of America. When Mrs. Roth retired to a less imposing residence in 1975 at the age of 85, the Filoli mansion and gardens were donated to the National Trust for Historic Preservation, which currently operates the estate.

The swimming pool was added to the estate in 1946, when the three Roth children really could enjoy it. Ninety feet long and thirty feet wide, the rectangular pool looks like a sky-blue gem in its setting of a red-brick border and green, flawlessly manicured lawn, flanked by a double row of stately, neatly trimmed yews. The pool is plastered white and ranges in depth from three to ten feet; the recirculated water is fed into it at water level, keeping the surface rippling constantly to cut down on glare.

At the south end of the pool stands a pool house with two dressing rooms, which also houses the pool equipment. Behind this pavilion are spectacular Sunburst Locusts and the Camperdown Elms that form a complete canopy of leaves during the summer.

The pool is no longer heated, although it is still used daily. The estate curator swims during the summer, and the garden superintendent uses it all year long—although she confesses to wearing a wet suit during the winter months!

The raised pool and the series of terraces around it promoted the idea
of the pool as architectural sculpture.

Thomas Church designed the pool using some of the same concepts apparent in the Modern house (not shown) at the end of the pool opposite the fountain.

According to noted landscape architect Garret Eckbo in a foreword to the 1995 edition of Thomas Church's *Gardens Are for People*, Church was "the last great traditional designer and the first modern designer." The pool Church designed and built in 1959 to accompany a residence south of San Francisco designed by the prominent architect William Wurster (1895–1973), Dean of Architecture and Planning at MIT (1944–50), is credited with originating features which set a significant trend in pool design.

Church originally intended to place the pool away from the house, but his client wanted the pool to be seen on the expanse of lawn in front of the house. The client had also admired the reflecting pools of European gardens, and suggested that the pool be raised above ground as they were. Church, who had once studied the gardens of Villa d'Este at Tivoli, designed a raised pool and tied it to the house with a spacious terrace. The transition from house to terrace to pool was made by continuing the terrazzo floors of the interior space onto the terrace outside, but setting the terrace squares diagonally to vary the appearance of the expanse of paving.

From the terrace, the raised, forty-by-twenty-foot pool extends to a platform at the far end, reached by three steps on either side of the pool. This platform holds a fountain which spills recirculated water into the pool in a small waterfall. Beyond the platform four steps lead up to a further elevated area containing a sculpture. These steps are of rough stone in contrast to the smooth terrazzo deck that borders the pool, denoting departure from the pool area, and a change in style and mood.

This sculptural pool, designed without the diving board and railed access steps common when it was built, set the tone for the following generation of pools, and introduced design features seen in today's pools, such as the Clarke pool in La Jolla (page 60).

The family pool on the Donnell Ranch in Sonoma is an extraordinary and justly famous swimming pool, its trend-setting design having held its own through decades of new developments in pool construction.

Old oaks frame the view and offer shade and protection from the wind.

The family pool on the Donnell Ranch in Sonoma is an extraordinary and justly famous swimming pool, its trend-setting design having held its own through decades of new developments in pool construction.

Designed by landscape architect Thomas Church in 1948 for Mr. and Mrs. Dewey Donnell, the pool is an architecturally important part of an extensive garden situated on a knoll with a breathtaking, thirty-mile panoramic view of the San Francisco Bay area. According to the designer, the free-form shape of the pool was inspired by the meandering creeks of the salt marshes below. This biomorphic shape has become emblematic of the new design outlook of the 1940s and 1950s, perhaps influenced by the art of Jean Arp and Joan Miró and public enthusiasm for new advances in biological research at the time. In his design Church took advantage of the versatility of the gunite process, which allows gunite to be sprayed onto a reinforced framework of almost any shape. Church's innovation has been adopted by other designers with varying degrees of success, and makers of mass-produced pools marketed the kidney-bean-shaped pool that occupied many yards in the 1960s and later. The remarkable success of the original Donnell pool, however, is based in part on the sensitive landscaping and the sinuous lines of the concrete, the lawn, and the water sculpture presenting a unified design.

The project was years in development and construction. In 1940 when the Donnell family bought the five-thousand-acre cattle ranch near Sonoma, they lived in an old ranch house while they rode the land on horseback seeking the best site on which to build what would become the family home. They enlisted Church's aid in selecting a site and choosing an architect for the house, and work was begun. Building material was scarce after World War II, but since the pool could be a valuable fire-fighting resource, supplies were made available and the pool complex was finished long before the main house. The Donnells moved into the pool house until the main residence was completed in 1952.

The pool design takes full advantage of the spectacular view, which is framed by stands of majestic oak trees that, along with banks of natural boulders, also provide a windbreak. A large natural rock was originally intended to form an island in the bend of the pool, but it was quickly realized that the rock's rough surface might injure swimmers who came too close. The island rock was therefore replaced by a smooth free-form concrete sculpture designed by sculptor Adaline Kent. On land the sculpture is balanced by a group of native rocks placed in a patch of grass that retraces the shape of the pool.

Within its shape, which was in the vanguard in 1948, the pool fills all requirements: a shallow area for children, sixty feet of unobstructed space for swimming, and a deep area for diving.

There is a shallow area for children to play; and although today few pools have diving boards, which are considered unsafe, the Donnell pool has a deep section for diving served by a conventional diving board. The pool offers sixty feet of unobstructed swimming and is plastered white, which allows the water to reflect the sky in shades of turquoise, and the spacious concrete deck around the pool is tan to reduce the glare of the sun.

In addition to the large original bathhouse, which now contains guest accommodations, a lanai offers shaded comfort by the pool. The lanai has two sides of sliding glass doors to take advantage of the view. When the doors are open the structure becomes part of the wide pool deck, and a long bench that follows the base of a rock wall into the enclosure provides plenty of seating. When the doors are closed and locked into a slot in the rock wall, the room can be heated by a fireplace on cold nights.

Each year designers and students, landscape architects and garden groups visit the Donnell pool. The present owners, the second generation of Donnells to own the ranch, honor the pledge made by the Donnell family almost fifty years ago to dedicate themselves to the maintenance and preservation of the pool as it was originally designed, and to resist any unnecessary and insensitive renovations.